C000285651

Discovering
the Secret
to a Successful

Prayer
Life

Discovering
the Secret
to a Successful

Prayer
Life

Suzette Hattingh

Copyright © 2008 - Suzette Hattingh

All rights reserved. This book is protected under the copyright laws. This book may not be copied or reprinted for commercial gain or profit. The use of short quotations or occasional page copying for personal or group study is permitted and encouraged. Permission will be granted upon request. Unless otherwise identified, Scripture quotations are from the New King James Version. Copyright © 1982 by Thomas Nelson, Inc. Used by permission. All rights reserved. Scripture quotations marked (KJV) are taken from the King James Version of the Bible, whose copyright ran out centuries ago. Its text is now in the public domain. Scripture quotations marked (NLT) are taken from the Holy Bible, New Living Translation, copyright © 1996. Used by permission of Tyndale House Publishers, Inc. Wheaton, Illinois 60189. All Rights Reserved. Scripture quotations marked (AMP) are taken from the Amplified® Bible, Copyright © 1954, 1958, 1962, 1964, 1965, 1987 by The Lockman Foundation. Used by permission. Emphasis within Scripture quotations is the author's own. Please note that Destiny Image Europe's publishing style capitalizes certain pronouns in Scripture that refer to the Father, Son, and Holy Spirit, and may differ from some Bible publishers' styles.

Take note that the name satan and related names are not capitalized. We choose not to acknowledge him, even to the point of violating grammatical rules.

DESTINY IMAGE™ EUROPE srl
Via Maiella, 1
66020 San Giovanni Teatino (Ch) - Italy

"Changing the world, one book at a time!"

This book and all other Destiny Image™ Europe books are available at Christian bookstores and distributors worldwide.

To order products, or for any other correspondence:

DESTINY IMAGE™ EUROPE srl
Via Acquacorrente, 6
65123 - Pescara - Italy
Tel. +39 085 4716623 - Fax: +39 085 9431270
E-mail: info@eurodestinyimage.com

Or reach us on the Internet: **www.eurodestinyimage.com**

ISBN: 978-88-89127-63-6
For Worldwide Distribution, Printed in the U.S.A.

1 2 3 4 5 6 7 8/13 12 11 10 09 08

Dedication

THIS BOOK IS DEDICATED TO the two people who have possibly impacted my life more than anybody else on this earth (with the exception of my own parents)—Reinhard and Anni Bonnke. What I am today, I owe much to them, and also to my coworker and close friend, Gayle Claxton, who has stood side by side with me for the past 20 years.

Endorsements

HAVE YOU EVER DESIRED TO be used of God in intercessory prayer? *Discovering the Secret to a Successful Prayer Life* is a practical "how to" manual, with a solid biblical foundation, to show how every person can be used of God in intercessory prayer. Intercession is not only for an "elect few," but is within the reach of every person. With clarity and honesty, Suzette Hattingh shows the battles, triumphs, and the great value of intercessory prayer and how it affects the world around us.

Randy Clark
President of Global Awakening
Author of *There is More!*

Every believer interested in living with eternal significance should read *Discovering the Secret to a Successful Prayer Life*. The lessons in this book were forged in the fires of romance with God and warfare against flesh and darkness. That unique combination will give the reader spiritual food that is both practical and profound. It will give the seasoned intercessor insight to go to the next level in obtaining breakthroughs. The beginner is given language for things that would otherwise take years to learn. And it is also a wake-up call for all those who think they are not called to a lifestyle of prayer. I truly want everyone I know to read *Discovering the Secret to a Successful Prayer Life.*

Bill Johnson
Pastor, Bethel Church, Redding, CA
Author, *When Heaven Invades Earth* and *Face to Face With God*

Suzette Hattingh's life itself is a testimony about the power of prayer. Every one of us who wants to learn how to press in through prayer and how to triumph victoriously will be changed by reading this book. This you can be sure of—with her unique humorous style, Suzette will challenge you in all kindness, and ignite, by the fire of the Holy Spirit, a new passion for prayer within you.

Jobst Bittner
Pastor, TOS Dienste

This book will change your life! This is not about reading something nice and pleasant—no, this book is about getting answers on how to develop a lifestyle of prayer. Suzette Hattingh writes what she lives and lives what she writes. Over decades, she truly has set marker stones all over the world through her anointed ministry of prayer and has walked before us as a role model. Now we have the privilege to press into a deeper level of a lifestyle of prayer. It is my desire that this book will soon be available in all churches in Germany and lead us into a true transformation.

Gerry Klein
Director, Bible School,
Christ for the Nations, Germany

I opened Suzette Hattingh's book, *Discovering the Secret to a Successful Prayer Life,* with the kind of joyous expectation one has on the way to a good cook's house for dinner. You know great care will have been taken in the preparation and presentation. Every flavor will be distinct, and when you are well satisfied, the recipes will be shared in detail that you may go and do likewise.

Suzette's book is her lifestyle by which she opens to the reader her very personal, practical prayer life for others to see and be able to follow.

Step-by-step she walks us through the Scriptures and teaches us how to use each one to put right our wrong concepts, to bring understanding to the often misunderstood ways that God leads and answers prayer. She has laid out a road map that will prove invaluable to those who will follow it carefully, for she has not only marked the high places, but also the dangerous blind spots and pitfalls to be avoided along the way.

This book, once read, will make clear the role of our constantly communicating Companion—the precious Holy Spirit. Without Him, prayer is just so much speech-making, but with Him, we are in conversation with God!

This book is about walking and talking with God, learning how to use the authority and take the dominion He has given to us. It's about seeing how to yield to the Holy Spirit's leading as He guides our prayers, sharing the burdens of Heaven with us on the earth. And it's about God in us, working through us, fulfilling His eternal purposes for us and for His Kingdom sake in all the earth.

Discovering the Secret to a Successful Prayer Life is not a classic for the bookcase, but a handbook for the road!

Charlene Harris
Missionary

While I was reading *Discovering the Secret to a Successful Prayer Life*, it literally felt like Suzette was sitting in our living room and preaching the written Word. And a friend, whom I had given the book to as a gift, told me very happily, that after having read Suzette's book, he now prays regularly with his wife—something that hadn't worked out in the past.

Manni Hohmann
Businessman

Discovering the Secret to a Successful Prayer Life is a fascinating book that combines biblical teachings with personal experience and a number of practical hints. And most of all, it encourages the reader to move on in prayer—step-by-step. This book for beginners as well as for advanced learners, makes prayer, with its many different facets, a personal adventure.

Ilona Piras
Translator

Table of Contents

Foreword

WHEN SUZETTE KNOCKED ON MY door and asked to be accepted as a team member in Christ for All Nations, at first I thought she was joking. She had been saved for only one year, and I had no idea of what slot she could fill in the ministry…but indeed a perfect position was waiting for her.

There was a need for a leader to establish a women's meeting in our gospel tent, and Suzette was just the one to fill it. In no time, she had the tent filled with ladies in the afternoons, with rivers of blessing flowing. Oh yes, intercession was also needed, and again, Suzette was the one to take it up. With awe, I watched her grow in the knowledge of the Word, taught by the Holy Spirit. She lived what she preached, a life totally clean and surrendered to Jesus. While I preached at crusades, fervent prayer rose up at the same time, with rivers of tears flowing for the lost. Suzette and her group of intercessors prayed through, and we reaped mighty harvests of souls.

After 17 years working side by side with me, Suzette had grown to be an excellent evangelist in her own right, and when I sent her from Frankfurt, Germany to Christchurch in New Zealand for meetings, I could feel her ministry tremors all the back to Europe! She soared as high as an eagle, and sometimes I felt that our wings were touching in midair.

"The time has come for you to start your own world ministry," I said to Suzette one day, "and I want to help you get it off the ground." Even though she was surprised by my remarks, Suzette seized the moment by founding *Voice in the City*, which has since developed into a worldwide ministry of excellence.

And now comes Suzette's new book, *Discovering the Secret to a Successful Prayer Life*. It is the best of the best, both revelation and revolution, simple but not simplistic. It penetrates the heart and should be read on one's knees. I highly recommend this book and Suzette Hattingh, an anointed handmaid of the Lord.

Reinhard Bonnke, Evangelist
Founder of Christ for All Nations (CfaN)

Introduction

As my eyes sweep across the overloaded bookshelf in my study and particularly at the numerous books on prayer that fill one shelf after another, my mind goes back to the many times in the past that I have read these books, desperately seeking the "how to" of prayer. Not that prayer can ever be a formula, yet how often had I read through those pages, and at the end of the book wondered, Where do I start? As well as, How can I reach the same place in the Spirit as those authors have?

Where do you start when witches dance around your hotel room during the night before a crusade begins? How do you encourage the Body of Christ to pray in preparation for the outreach, when they are too fearful even to mention the name of satan, because they are scared that misfortune will come their way? How do you break through when you are all alone, and then remain in victory even when it seems that the heavens are like brass and all hell is breaking loose around you? Or how do you inspire your prayer group and make prayer an exciting adventure for them, when they seem to be so uninterested?

Having led the prayer ministry for Reinhard Bonnke's crusades in *Christ for All Nations* around the world for 14 years, and later, founding my own missions organization, *Voice in the City*, has taught me the adventures, battles, and victories of passionate intercessory prayer. And now, my goal for this book is to make intercession so practical that everyone who reads it can close it at the end and say, "I can do that as well!" I want to take the mystique out of prayer and make it an attainable and exciting lifestyle.

This book is something you can use as a prayer manual, a teaching guide, as well as an inspiration to propel your prayer life into new dimensions. Welcome to the adventure...

Suzette Hattingh
Founder of *Voice in the City*

CHAPTER 1

Biblical Foundation for Intercession

*He is like a man building a house, who dug deep and laid **the foundation on the rock**. And when the flood arose, the stream beat vehemently against that house, and could not shake it, for **it was founded on the rock*** (Luke 6:48).

*They drank of that spiritual Rock that followed them, **and that Rock was Christ*** (1 Corinthians 10:4b).

*For **no other foundation** can anyone lay than that which is laid, which is **Jesus Christ*** (1 Corinthians 3:11).

IN THIS CHAPTER WE WILL be studying intercession. And although we will not be studying languages, an understanding of particular words and what they mean will help us to explore the significance of what has been written. The Bible was written in two languages—the Old Testament in Hebrew and the New Testament in Greek. When the various meanings are understood, a richer and deeper understanding of the Scriptures is the outcome. Hence, we will build our solid foundation based solely upon the Word of God.

WORDS AND DEFINITIONS

The word *intercession* is our main and most important word through-out this book. We have several examples of intercessors in the Word of God, including Esther, Nehemiah, Moses, David, and many others. They were tremendous intercessors and wonderful men and women of prayer; however, the first reference in the Bible to the word "interces-sion" does not occur until Isaiah 53:12, which reads:

> *Therefore I will divide Him a portion with the great, and He shall divide the spoil with the strong, because He poured out His soul unto death, and He was numbered with the transgressors, and He bore the sin of many, and made **intercession** for the transgressors* (Isaiah 53:12).

VINE'S	STRONG'S
To collide with	To invade
To encroach upon	To come in between
To drive in	To entreat
To strike against	To meet together
To be violent against	Intercession; to pray
	To be a peacemaker

The word "intercession" in Hebrew is *paga*, which is pronounced "paw-gah." There are many shades of meaning to this word, and we will look at several of these definitions found in the Vine's and Strong's Dictionaries.

The first definition, ***"to collide with"*** is similar to two cars meeting head-on, resulting in a mighty crash. When two forces come against each other, you have some concept of the word *paga*.

Another definition, ***"to encroach upon"*** can be related to an animal hunting for prey. My country of birth is South Africa, where I grew up understanding the way that lions hunt animals. When a lion is searching for prey, it actually *encroaches* upon that prey. What does that mean? The lion waits until it sees an animal that is isolated and separated from the rest of the herd. Gradually, the lion encroaches on the prey's territory, moving closer and closer, until suddenly, it pounces, jumps on top of the animal, and drops it to the ground for the kill. The word *encroach* means "to come in with force upon a situation." It literally means "to put on a hook, or to hook on."

The next definition of *intercession* is **"to drive in."** In order to put a nail into a piece of wood, the nail must be hit with a few sharp blows of a hammer. That force through the hammer pushes the nail through the wood.

Intercession can also mean **"to strike against,"** or **"to be violent against."** This violence has nothing to do with physical action. It actually means to rise up from within, with a determination before the Lord to reclaim your spiritual inheritance or land that has already been won for you on Calvary.

Are you getting a feel for what this amazing, wonderful word *paga* signifies? It is an action word; there is nothing passive about intercession. It is like a double-edged sword—both edges are sharp and effective, cutting in opposite directions yet administered together through the blade. The previous definitions represent the one edge in action—rising up, moving forward, a powerful force. Now let's consider the other edge, one that is completely different, almost like a paradox.

The first definition of the other side of intercession is **"to invade."** When a country is invaded, enemy forces spread throughout the land. Likewise, when bacteria infects a body, it multiplies and spreads out as far as possible. In other words, it is a moving in and a spreading out.

The next definition is **"to come in between."** We all understand the concept of coming in between, like a referee between two boxers or a wedge placed in a log before it is split in half. An intercessor is just like that; he comes in between two opposing situations, filling the gap on behalf of both to make the situation whole.

"To entreat" is the next definition, which means to ask for or to request earnestly. Think of a small child who persists in asking his mother for a favor. He never seems to give up until that request is granted. Another definition is **"to meet together."** The prophet Amos portrayed this idea simply: "Can two walk together, unless they have agreed?" (Amos 3:3). Each of these wonders of *intercession* and their various facets will be discussed in subsequent chapters.

When we think of **intercession and prayer**, we can describe intercession as a partnership with God. It signifies a coming together with Him in order to do that which He wants to do. You are never alone as you pray with Jesus and the Holy Spirit who seek the heart of the Father to bring to fulfillment what He wants to accomplish on the earth. In addition, as a **peacemaker**, your whole purpose of coming in between and working together with Almighty God in partnership is to resolve a situation, so that a godly peace will result and that His will may be done.

All of the previous definitions and descriptions of the word *paga* give us a true understanding of what is meant by *intercession*. In addition, we need to know that there are two main actions of intercession:

1. Warfare—facing satan or the oppressive forces, in the name of Jesus, on behalf of a person or a situation. This represents one edge of the double-edged sword.

2. Travail—facing the Father, on behalf of a person or situation, through weeping, prayer, and pleading for that person or situation. This represents the opposite edge of the sword.

IT IS THE FACT THAT ONE PRAYS, THAT MOVES THE HEART OF GOD.

To say that prayer as a part of intercession has power is an understatement. Indeed, I believe that prayer moves mountains, and that combined prayer moves nations and cities. It is prayer that unlocks the spirit realm.

I firmly believe that there is a special place for certain people to lock themselves away and to pray for hours, weeks, or even months—a time and place where they are fully engaged in pouring themselves out in prayer. And we are honored and blessed to have such people in our day. However, there are many people who think that an intercessor can only be this person who has withdrawn from society and who spends all day in the Holy of Holies, like Moses in a face-to-face conversation with God.

But that is not so. Although I am a world intercessor, I cannot say that I lock myself away for hours or days at a time. I simply do not have time for that. The demands of my ministry, my teaching schedules, and even my personal lifestyle do not allow for it. Nevertheless, I do pray a lot at night, or whenever I can fit in the time! It is most important for you to understand that it is not the quantity of prayer, not even the quality of prayer, but the fact that one prays, that moves the heart of God.

Intercession is not something that is turned on and off, like a light switch; it is not even a prayer meeting, although it can be part of a prayer meeting. It is an ongoing, evolving, understanding of the Father-heart, which produces two significant results—standing in the gap and changing the land.

STANDING IN THE GAP

So I sought for a man among them who would make a wall, and **stand in the gap** *before Me on behalf of the land, that I should not destroy it; but I found no one* (Ezekiel 22:30).

This Scripture is one of the best examples in the Word of God of an intercessor—one who stands in the gap. In this verse, the person seeking for someone to stand in the gap is the Lord, and we are the ones who should respond to the need.

The state of our lands and nations rests on the shoulders of those who pray, no matter what politicians and statesmen might think or say. Almighty God has clearly stated that we are to protect the land, so that He will not destroy it on account of its abominations and unrighteousness.

I would like to share something personal with you, about how the Lord dealt with me concerning this matter. One day, upon arriving home after watching one of the "Transformation" videos, I became increasingly disturbed. Watching that video had forced me consider the state of the countries affected. They all had been virtually destroyed; their economies were in ruins, righteousness could not be found anywhere, and they were in deep trouble. Most of our countries in the world now come under one of the headings of "poor economy," "rampant unrighteousness," or "ruled by corruption." And I was feeling troubled and anxious to know what to do.

During my prayers for the nations, I asked, "God, how must I now pray? Does this mean that a country has to be destroyed before we can have revival? Should I pray, 'Lord, shake the economy, let the destruction continue so that we can have revival'?" I really struggled with this problem. I said again to the Lord, "I need a word from You, because what is the use of praying and fasting for 40 days here or 30 days there, holding prayer meetings or national conventions, when it seems that only those countries that are totally broken down seem to experience a move of God in transformation and revival?" Soon, however, I understood that God is not moved by the economy or ungodly principles; rather, *He is moved by prayer.*

GARMENTS OF SALVATION AND A ROBE
OF RIGHTEOUSNESS

Almighty God is looking for someone to build a hedge or fence of righteousness again, which guards the land. Why does He need someone? So that He, the righteous God, can bless the land in response to our prayers rather than destroy the land as a result of righteously judging sin. He is the God of love, the God of mercy, the God of grace, the God of salvation, and the God of healing. And He is also the God of righteousness.

> *Now this is His name by which He will be called: the Lord our righteousness* (Jeremiah 23:6b).

He is Jehovah Tsidkenu, and He must judge sin. Therefore, when He says, "Stand in the gap before Me on behalf of the land, that I should not destroy it," He is expressing His desire to protect and bless the land rather than ruin it; yet even so, He has to deal with sin.

This is where the intercessor comes in—the one who will "stand in the gap." This does not mean that intercessors are perfect, or that they do not make mistakes. By no means! It means that we stand in the gap, clothed with the garments of salvation and covered with the robe of righteousness, both of which are imputed to us by the Lord Jesus Christ. In addition, as intercessors we can draw from His character on behalf of the land. So often the intercessors in the Bible prayed the character of God. In other words, the acknowledgment of His attributes were their very prayers, much more than presenting the needs of the land.

> *I will greatly rejoice in the Lord, my soul shall be joyful in my God; for He has clothed me with the **garments of salvation**, He has covered me with the **robe of righteousness**, as a bridegroom decks himself with ornaments, and as a bride adorns herself with her jewels* (Isaiah 61:10).

We are made righteous in Christ Jesus:

Yet indeed I also count all things loss for the excellence of the knowledge of Christ Jesus my Lord, for whom I have suffered the loss of all things, and count them as rubbish, that I may gain Christ and be found in Him, not having my own righteousness, which is from the law, but that which is through faith in Christ, the righteousness which is from God by faith (Philippians 3:8-9).

These Scriptures help us understand the right or the authority that we have as children of God to stand in the gap before the Lord on behalf of others. The intercessor has a responsibility as well as the power and authority to stand in the gap. He has this responsibility because of his adornment—the garment of salvation and the robe of righteousness. Only those who are born again are given this adornment to wear and therefore are able to stand before a righteous God. The power and authority comes only through salvation.

*Be anxious for nothing, but in everything by prayer and supplication, with thanksgiving, **let your requests be made known to God*** (Philippians 4:6).

Let us therefore come boldly to the throne of grace, *that we may obtain mercy and find grace to help in time of need* (Hebrews 4:16).

Intercessors are able to create the required "spiritual wall" around the land and can "stand in the gap" or fill the need, where this wall of righteousness is failing, thereby plugging the breach. To use another analogy, you and I are like a bridge that is required to span a river; we link one side with the other. This is an incredible privilege that God has granted us. All the time that we are standing in the gap against the enemy, the Lord is working on the restoration of the land.

GOD HAS SENT A MEDIATOR

In the Old Testament, Job addressed the subject of intercession. He acknowledged God's justice and claimed that there is no contending with Him.

Nor is there any mediator between us, who may lay his hand on us both. Let Him take His rod away from me, and do not let dread of Him terrify me (Job 9:33-34).

Job said, in effect, "I wish that there was someone who could stand before God on my behalf, and before me on God's behalf, and who could be a mediator."

Praise God, there is now such a Person—the Lord Jesus Christ!

For there is one God and one Mediator between God and men, **the Man Christ Jesus** (1 Timothy 2:5).

Jesus the Mediator *of the new covenant* (Hebrews 12:24a).

Thank God, when Jesus hung between Heaven and earth, He became the perfect bridge to connect Heaven with earth and earth with Heaven.

As children of God, we stand in partnership with Jesus in the gap so that the plan of God for that situation can be fulfilled. This is a wonderful truth, and one of the glorious facts about intercession. I want you to rise up in your spirits, and to start enjoying intercession. Praying is an exciting business. Admittedly, there are times when it indeed requires perseverance, but it is still wonderfully glorious, because you are never alone. Let me emphasize that last point—*you are never alone.* You are in partnership with Christ before the Father!

For we are **God's fellow workers** (1 Corinthians 3:9a).

(Actually, I am jumping ahead of myself, as you are going to learn how to become a partner with the Most High God in the next chapter. This is a bit like the hors d'oeuvres before the main course!)

AS CHILDREN OF GOD, WE STAND IN PARTNERSHIP WITH JESUS IN THE GAP SO THAT THE PLAN OF GOD FOR THAT SITUATION CAN BE FULFILLED.

Jesus is seated at the right hand of the Father making intercession for us.

Who is he who condemns? It is Christ who died, and furthermore is also risen, who is even **at the right hand of God***, who also makes intercession for us* (Romans 8:34).

The Holy Spirit is also active on our behalf. He also is making intercession for us!

*Likewise the Spirit also helps in our weaknesses. For we do not know what we should pray for as we ought, but **the Spirit Himself makes intercession for us** with groanings which cannot be uttered* (Romans 8:26).

GOD WILL TAKE US TO THAT PLACE OF PRAYER, WHERE HE WILL MOLD US SO THAT CHRIST IS FORMED INSIDE US.

Therefore, every single time that you start to pray, you have company! Both Jesus and the Holy Spirit are making intercession for you and with you. Now, you may feel that you are not breaking through or as if the heavens are as bronze; however, never, ever let your feelings dictate to you, when you are dealing with Almighty God.

The truth of the matter is that you *are in partnership with God*, no matter how you feel. You are a coworker with the Almighty!

Paul, in his letter to the Galatians, had this to say:

My little children, for whom I labor in birth [travail, intercession] *again until Christ is formed in you* [until the process is done] (Galatians 4:19).

What Paul is telling us in this passage is very important for intercessors to understand. He states that God is more interested in His character in us than He is in our performance. God will take us to that place of prayer, and like a potter, He will mold, bend, and shape us so that Christ is formed inside us. Paul boldly exclaimed, "...until Christ shall have been formed in you" (literal translation).

From this Scripture, we can understand that God's entire plan is to bring blessing, not destruction, which is precisely what Ezekiel 22:30 is telling us. We have a God of love, and a God of blessings and mercy; yet He is also a just and righteous God, which is why it is so important that you and I stand in the gap in our own weaknesses and shortcomings, yet clothed in His garments of righteousness. This is what I find so awesome about intercession—the omnipotent, omniscient God, who can do all things, wants to include you and me, so *that together with* Him, we are able to influence world issues and conduct world evangelism, simply by our prayers.

Intercession—A Partnership

It must be restated—intercession is not something that can be switched on and off. The lifestyle of intercession comes only out of a relationship with God, which means that He can call on you 24/7, just as He pleases.

In this relationship, God intends us to live in a lifestyle of intercession and prayer. It is not a matter of trying to convince God to answer us, as if we have to break through to Heaven to pull down the answer. Believe me, He is more eager to answer than we are to pray! It pleases Him to answer our prayer.

For the Lord takes pleasure in His people (Psalm 149:4a).

He takes pleasure in answering His people. Therefore, we need to understand that intercession is not coming to God in order to convince Him to do something; we are not trying to twist His arm so that He will give in to our demands. Intercession is praying that which is on the heart of the Father, as He touches your heart with what is touching His.

"But Suzette," you say, "I'm not at that place."

Indeed, I did not get at that place overnight. I too had to learn. I had to learn how to walk with Him, move with Him, and how to be more sensitive to the voice of God. It is a process that takes time. It is just like learning to walk—the first steps (which are always worship) are wobbly and unsure. Nevertheless, in time, you no longer remember the bumps and falls, but look forward to that anticipated walk of confidence.

True prayer starts in the heart of the Father. It always originates with Him. It then becomes a circle. It comes from the Father's heart, through Jesus, who is at the right hand of the Father, and by the Holy Spirit, who indwells us. We are the temples of the Holy Spirit, so that by the time you begin to feel a burden to pray for something, half of the circle has been completed. You now begin to pray. Together with Jesus and the Holy Spirit, you bring it before the Father, where it originated, and He answers it.

So shall My word be that goes forth from My mouth; it shall not return to Me void, but it shall accomplish what I please, and it shall prosper in the thing for which I sent it (Isaiah 55:11).

Thus, the full circle of intercession looks like the following graphic.

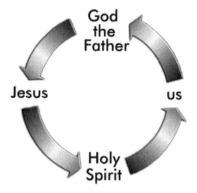

*Now **He who searches the hearts knows what the mind of the Spirit is,** because He makes intercession for the saints according to the will of God. And we know that all things work together for good to those who love God, to those who are the called according to His purpose* (Romans 8:27-28).

The Holy Spirit intercedes and pleads before God on behalf of the saints, according to, and in harmony with the will of God. Intercession originates with God! Child of God, you are one of those "who are the called according to His purpose"; it is a partnership, and a partnership in which all things work together for good.

The word *partnership* is used in almost every chapter of this book because that is what prayer is all about. We are partners or coworkers with God in prayer. The following diagram shows the formation of this partnership.

THE HOLY SPIRIT, OUR HELPER

Also, in Romans 8:26, there is a wonderful word that describes the Holy Spirit. He "helps" us.

> Likewise **the Spirit also helps** in our weaknesses. For we do not know what we should pray for as we ought, but the Spirit Himself makes intercession for us with groanings which cannot be uttered (Romans 8:26).

"Help" is a rare word in the Bible, and is used only twice in the New Testament. In Romans 8:26, it shows the significance of the Holy Spirit in us. The other occurrence is in the Gospel of Luke, where it is used in connection with Martha and Mary.

> But Martha was distracted with much serving, and she approached Him and said, "Lord, do You not care that my sister has left me to serve alone? Therefore tell her to help me" (Luke 10:40).

Almighty God is so concerned that our prayers have impact that He sent the best possible help—the Holy Spirit, the third Person of the Blessed Trinity! He could not send anyone or anything better, because by His Spirit, He came Himself.

The Holy Spirit is our helper. This word "helps" is a translation of the Greek *sun-anti-lambanomai*, which has the following meanings:

- To lay hold along with, to strive to obtain with others, help in obtaining.

- To take hold with another.

The Greek word is made up of three separate parts, indicated by the hyphens:

Sun—together with.

Anti—against.

Lambanomai comes from a primary verb *lambano*—to boldly take hold of, or to catch.

Putting all this together shows us that we, *together with* the Holy Spirit, take hold of something in prayer, *against* a problem. I have italicized the words "together with," because this is most important. We cannot do it on our own. Almighty God uses us as a means whereby a certain action is accomplished. It is an act of partnership, cooperation, and coworking.

As a way of illustration, let me tell you a story I heard from Reinhard Bonnke, which explains this partnership in a wonderful way.

There was a large elephant, ambling its way through the African countryside. He was not headed anywhere in particular but was simply strolling along in search of food. Soon, he came to a bridge and started to cross to the other side. As the elephant lumbered across the bridge, the structure began to groan, swinging to the right and to the left. Unperturbed, the elephant slowly moved forward.

Meanwhile, behind the ear of the elephant sat a tiny ant as the larger animal crossed the swinging bridge. When they both reached the other side, the ant said to the elephant, "Elephant, you and I together, we really made that bridge swing, didn't we!"

If I may put it reverently, Jesus is the elephant, and you are the ant. You, together with God, get things done. *Together with against*—it may not be grammatical, but it conveys the whole spirit of intercession.

The last part of our long Greek word is *lambano*—a taking hold of. What a glorious concept this now becomes. When we considered the Hebrew word *paga*, we learned of the following meanings—to come in between, to entreat, to meet together, to intercede, to pray, to be a peacemaker. Well, this is precisely what we have now. Together with Christ, together with the Holy Spirit, we are in partnership, and we are taking hold of a situation. We are taking hold of it in prayer and in fasting—*together with against*.

One day, the Lord spoke to me and said, "Suzette, you walk in unbelief!" At that time, I had been praying about a specific matter and was pressing in but still did not see the answer. The Lord said to me, "Suzette, come into that place of worship. Come into that place of pressing in *with Me*. Come into that place, and understand that you are *not alone* there. You do not need to convince Me; I am convinced about this issue in My Word."

Child of God, we do not have to convince God! He is *together with against*. I understood then that much of my effort came from my own strength and ability. I simply cried out to the Lord for forgiveness and said, "Lord, help me. You know what I am like. You will have to mold me and teach me how to press in, but only together with the Holy Spirit, and with what is on His heart."

And that is what the Lord began to do. He started to teach and train me, and gradually, I began to move with the Holy Spirit and to move with what was on the heart of God. I became sensitive to what He wanted, rather than what I wanted. I made mistakes of course; we all make mistakes, but Almighty God does not fall off His throne if we make a mistake! Again, watch a baby as he learns to walk. In the beginning, he falls over more times than he moves forward. However, watch that same baby after he has practiced many times, and one day, you will have to move fast to catch him!

INTERCESSION IS A MINISTRY OF REST, PEACE, AND LOVE

We must stop striving in our own ability, and enter into the rest of Almighty God, especially through worship. Although more about this subject will be discussed in a subsequent chapter, at this point I want to share the following Scripture:

> There remains therefore **a rest for the people of God**. For he who has entered His rest has himself also **ceased from his works** as God did from His. Let us therefore be diligent to enter that rest (Hebrews 4:9-11a).

Be at ease, child of God, when you start to feel a burden or a need to pray for someone—Jesus already has the matter in hand. He and the Holy Spirit are already praying about it, and you have been brought into the circle so that *together with against*, the matter can be resolved.

Although this has tremendous power, it is very important to realize that through our prayers, we are not allowed to control another person's life. You cannot control your pastor, leadership, or loved ones by your intercession. Control is never of God. Jesus never controlled; He reigned. To reign with Christ is something completely different than trying to control.

We are there to support, to encourage, to exhort, but not to enforce our own way through our prayer, no matter how spiritual it might sound.

When God begins to show you things about others, you will see both the best and the worst in the same person. You will see things concerning people that others may have no idea about. If God allows you to see with His eyes by means of discernment or revelation, it must be treated as holy. That is not the time to start a gossip campaign under the wonderful false mantle of concern. Do not reveal what God has shown you. It is a personal matter between you and Him. Remember, this is partnership, sharing the secrets of God's heart.

True intercession is a ministry of love, and love covers a multitude of sin.

> *And above all things have fervent love for one another, for "love will cover a multitude of sins"* (1 Peter 4:8).

As we conclude this first chapter, consider the following:

> *Now the fruit of righteousness is sown in peace by those who make peace* (James 3:18).

Those who make peace are peacemakers, and, as they sow in peace, the resulting harvest (the fruit of that sowing) is righteousness. What is the Lord looking for in order to protect the land? He looks for righteousness to replace the unrighteousness of that land. Peacemakers, who are sowing peace, harvest the fruit of righteousness.

DO NOT REVEAL WHAT GOD HAS SHOWN YOU. IT IS A PERSONAL MATTER BETWEEN YOU AND HIM.

Intercessors stand in the gap, sowing peace, so that *together with against*, with Jesus and the Holy Spirit, the situation is grasped and resolved in accordance with the wishes of the Father.

CHAPTER 2

The Harvest of Intercession

INTERCESSION RESULTS IN A TWOFOLD blessing. First, the Lord answers the petition; and second, a blessing is bestowed on the intercessor—the intercessor's personal harvest. Suppose you intercede for a friend to receive salvation, and after a certain time, that friend is born again. This is the primary blessing resulting from your intercession. There is also a secondary blessing—the personal harvest resulting from that prayer.

It is important to emphasize a fundamental truth here. We do not give in order to receive. We give because we love. Even when we know that there is no personal gain to be had in our giving, we simply give.

When we pray to the Father on behalf of another, we pray because we love our Lord. We are His servants carrying out His wishes. We do not pray for others in the hope of a personal blessing. However, because God cares for His children, He delights to bless them out of His abundance. We can never out-give God, not even in prayer.

The fundamental law of seedtime and harvest takes effect in intercession. It is a spiritual law as well as a law of nature.

> While the earth remains, **seedtime and harvest**, cold and heat, winter and summer, and day and night shall not cease (Genesis 8:22).

*Even as I have seen, those who plow iniquity and **sow** trouble **reap** the same* (Job 4:8).

*He who continually goes forth weeping, bearing **seed for sowing**, shall doubtless come again with rejoicing, bringing his **sheaves** with him* (Psalm 126:6).

*Do not be deceived, God is not mocked; for **whatever a man sows, that he will also reap**. For he who sows to his flesh will of the flesh reap corruption, but **he who sows to the Spirit will of the Spirit reap everlasting life*** (Galatians 6:7-8).

GOD IS THE GOD OF THE HARVEST; AND IT IS IN HIS TIME THAT THE HARVEST IS REAPED.

In the scriptural examples above, both the natural and the spiritual significance of sowing and reaping are given. It is virtually impossible to pray and not reap a harvest. God is the God of the harvest; it is one of His many attributes, but it is in His time and not in ours that the harvest is reaped.

Sowing and reaping are very much like computers—what goes in, must come out. In other words, if you want to reap maize, you will not plant bananas. Whatever you plant in your spirit grows and comes out multiplied in the harvest. Sow hate, and you will be hateful and hated. Sow love, and you will be loving and loved. If you sow intercession, prayer, and evangelism, you will reap a Holy Spirit explosion. (More detail is provided in a subsequent chapter.) It is a very simple, straightforward law.

PASSION

In order to produce a bountiful spiritual harvest, we need passion. We need to be ***passionate people of prayer***. What does that mean? What is passionate prayer? It is prayer that comes from the heart of a

FOOTBALL FANS SHOW GREAT PASSION.

person and not just from his brain via his mouth. It is prayer that comes from the whole person—spirit, soul, and body. That does not mean that it has to be loud and lengthy. A short one-liner from the heart is more effective than a whole essay of round-the-world prayer said to impress those gathered at the prayer meeting. Passion is a love that consumes the whole person. Just watch the fans at a football game when their team scores—that is passion. Likewise, we need to have that kind of passion about our Lord and Savior, about the works that He has done, and about the works that He wants us to do; and then we will become passionate people of prayer.

PENETRATION

Not only do we have to be passionate in prayer, but we also need to press in, to penetrate into the situation with the Gospel of Jesus Christ.

Many people become discouraged when, after much prayer and intercession, there appears to be no resolution to the problem. They continue to ask God to resolve the problem, yet they never give Him an opportunity to do so. For example, if you want to pray for your city, then you also need to be doing something whereby God can bring in the answer. Create an opportunity for the answer. Get out there and start talking to the lost. Start presenting the Gospel so that the Lord can cause a breakthrough as the result of your prayers.

I have often thought how I would like to radically change many a midweek prayer meeting. Instead of the usual (excuse me for the expression) "hymn-sandwich" with a few prayer points as the filling, I would arrange for some buses to be parked outside the church an hour before the prayer meeting. I would ask all the prayers to come to the meeting an hour earlier and to get onto the buses. Then, we would visit the railway stations, the universities, the entertainment areas of the city, the discos, and the cinemas. Then we would move on into the more deprived areas where the drug-pushers, prostitutes, and other youngsters are selling themselves on the streets. Finally, we would return to the prayer meeting, and, having seen the reality of the city, I would say, "Now, let us pray!"

Most of us live in comfortable isolation from the reality of the world, and even if we live within that reality, we move around as though we wear blinders, seeing nothing to the right or to the left. My personal testimony will highlight the point that I am making.

One Christmas Eve, many years ago, a few of us decided to go into the city, to a place where some of the homeless usually gather, to hold a blessing. Now, whether it was because it was so cold, or the fact that it was Christmas Eve, I do not know, but there was no one in that area. So,

~

CREATE AN OP-
PORTUNITY FOR
THE ANSWER.

~

we decided to split into smaller groups to see if we could distribute our gifts elsewhere.

Hearing the sound of many voices in the park, my companion and I decided to go there. We had not gone far when suddenly I felt an object being forced into my back. Instantly, I knew that it was a gun! Let me remind you that this was not some Third World city but my hometown of Frankfurt! I then slowly turned around to face two men.

"What do you want?" asked one of them.

By the grace of God, I had an immediate answer. "Nothing that you've got. But you might like what I've got—Christmas gifts."

"Is that all?" he replied.

"Yes."

Without realizing it, in my innocence, I had stumbled into a drug ring. Here they were, young and old alike, warming their heroin on little spoons, injecting themselves, and selling themselves for more drugs. I had walked into a world completely unknown to me.

As I looked around, I thought, *Oh, my God, where have I landed!* His response was immediate, *Where is the Church?*

That night, I realized what a hypocrite I had been. Although I had prayed and prayed, moving from one prayer meeting to another, spending most of my time in intercession or in the intercession hall; yet 20 minutes from my home, I had walked into what I can only call a scene from hell. It brought me back to reality, and I went home, crying like a child, amazed that I could have been so blind. How could I have been so "super-spiritual" and yet know nothing of what was going on around me? At that time, I thought that evangelism was the responsibility of somebody else. However, that night changed my life forever!

I never thought that God could use me to reach souls for Him. I had been a prayer only. But that night, I made a promise to the Lord: "You send them to me, and by Your grace I will speak up no matter what." At first it was difficult. I did not even know how to approach people, but today I am an interceding evangelist, conducting my own crusades worldwide, because of one cold winter's night in a Frankfurt park.

EVANGELISM IS NOT A SUGGESTION—IT IS A COMMAND

Intercession and evangelism are inseparable from one another. Jesus did not come to this world so that we could have pleasant prayer gatherings, enjoyable church meetings, or conferences in comfortable buildings. He came for a sick and dying world! For that reason, to the level that we pray, we must also reach out.

> *And He said to them, "Go into all the world and **preach the gospel** to every creature"* (Mark 16:15).

> ***Preach the word!** Be ready in season and out of season. Convince, rebuke, exhort, with all longsuffering and teaching* (2 Timothy 4:2).

Not all are called to speak to hundreds of thousands, but all of us can speak to one. He might not have called you to be a preacher, but He has called everyone to be a witness.

> *But you shall receive power when the Holy Spirit has come upon you; and **you shall be witnesses to Me** in Jerusalem, and in all Judea and Samaria, and to the end of the earth* (Acts 1:8).

That is the penetration with evangelism. I believe that if you cut true *intercession* out of your program and life, you will virtually cut the "lifeline." Moreover, if you cut *evangelism* out of your program and life, you will miss your first calling "to be a witness," and believe me, spiritual drought will set in.

The foundation of all true intercession is the cross of Calvary. For that reason, intercession can never be an end in itself, but a means to an end. The atoning sacrifice of Jesus is the basis for all intercession for a lost and dying world.

PERSEVERANCE

An intercessor must continue earnestly in prayer and intercession before the Lord and persevere until the breakthrough is achieved.

> ***Continue earnestly in prayer**, being vigilant in it with thanksgiving* (Colossians 4:2).

> ***Let us continue to go and pray before the Lord**, and seek the Lord of hosts…* (Zechariah 8:21b).

(More about this subject is found in Chapter Seven, "A Burden and How to Pray It Through.")

GIVE, AND IT WILL BE GIVEN

But this I say: He who sows sparingly will also reap sparingly, and he who sows bountifully will also reap bountifully (2 Corinthians 9:6).

A literal translation of the latter portion of this text reads:

He who sows in blessings, in blessings shall also reap.

You must certainly have noticed that this text is usually only used at the time of the offering, with a reference only to money. However, this spiritual and natural law applies to many areas in life. Just so that you understand the whole of Paul's argument on this point, let's look at the entire text.

But this I say: He who sows sparingly will also reap sparingly, and he who sows bountifully will also reap bountifully. So let each one give as he purposes in his heart, not grudgingly or of necessity; for God loves a cheerful giver. And God is able to make all grace abound toward you, that you, always having all sufficiency in all things, may have an abundance for every good work. As it is written: "He has dispersed abroad, He has given to the poor; His righteousness endures forever." **Now may He who supplies seed to the sower, and bread for food, supply and multiply the seed you have sown and increase the fruits of your righteousness,** *while you are enriched in everything for all liberality, which causes thanksgiving through us to God. For the administration of this service not only supplies the needs of the saints, but also is abounding through many thanksgivings to God, while, through the proof of this ministry, they glorify God for the obedience of your confession to the gospel of Christ, and for your liberal sharing with them and all men, and by their prayer for you, who long for you because of the exceeding grace of God in you. Thanks be to God for His indescribable gift!* (2 Corinthians 9:6-15)

Verse 10, which is emphasized in bold, has special significance in our case as an intercessor. In the last chapter, we mentioned that a peacemaker who sows in peace will reap a harvest of righteousness; and

I want to point out here as well as in the earlier Scripture, Paul prays for God to *"increase the fruits of your righteousness."*

Next, let's consider part of Luke's narrative of the Sermon on the Mount where Jesus said:

> **Give, and it will be given to you***: good measure, pressed down, shaken together, and running over will be put into your bosom. For with the same measure that you use, it will be measured back to you* (Luke 6:38).

"Give...and it will be given!" The strength of these words is in the command "Give." We are to give as commanded by the Lord. But, having given, then comes the promise—"...and it will be given"—no "ifs" or "buts"—"Give, and it will be given."

What is meant by "the same measure"? Well, if you sow hate, you will certainly reap hate so much more. Sow criticism, and you will reap it—30, 60, or a 100 fold! Give love, and you will be bathed in love. Pour out empathy; subsequently, you will receive floods in return. This also certainly applies to prayer—you pray for others, others pray for you. All of these returns are "pressed down, shaken together, running over." There are no empty spaces, no corners where the blessing will not reach. This is God's promise to those who give!

When Jesus hung on the cross, He did not pay part of the price; He paid the full price for the restoration of the entire man to make us whole. He gave everything He had—His life! That is why He could make that final cry—"It is finished." The English language does not do the Greek justice here. The words really mean, "Paid in full!" Our debtor's account has been paid in full, which is why, when we give, we too must give our all. There can be no holding back.

THE SEEDS OF PRAYER

In applying these thoughts to our prayer life, what exactly does it mean? Actually, it is very simple. We give prayer, and we will be given prayer—not more subjects to pray about, but prayer directed to us individually.

Every single prayer that you pray is a seed. That seed is planted in the spiritual harvest fields of God, where it falls to the ground and produces in abundance.

The kingdom of God is as if a man should scatter seed on the ground, and should sleep by night and rise by day, and the seed should sprout and grow, he himself does not know how (Mark 4:26-27).

It is like a mustard seed, which a man took and put in his garden; and it grew and became a large tree, and the birds of the air nested in its branches (Luke 13:19).

Most assuredly, I say to you, unless a grain of wheat falls into the ground and dies, it remains alone; but if it dies, it produces much grain (John 12:24).

EVERY SINGLE PRAYER THAT YOU PRAY IS A SEED, WHICH IS PLANTED IN THE SPIRITUAL HARVEST FIELDS OF GOD.

The more you pray for others, the more others will pray for you. This is the intercessor's personal harvest. Knowing the power of this principle, we make sure that in our offices, our staff pray twice a week for the nations as well as for those who write to us with prayer requests. Our ministry needs prayer, but in order for us to draw a harvest in prayer, we first have to sow!

Nevertheless, we are human and the "I, my, me, mine" syndrome can often creep in. Most of us pray for our families, our needs, and our church, which is as it should be. But when do we ever change the subject, and pray for the family next door and their needs, pray for the church down the road and their problems? Once we begin to realize what God wants us to pray for, then the time of prayer becomes too short. What used to be a struggle to get through an hour, now cannot be completed in an evening. When we cast our net wide, God will soon fill it to overflowing.

*And He said to them, "Cast the net on the right side of the boat, and you will find some." So they cast, and now **they were not able to draw it in because of the multitude of fish*** (John 21:6).

As I began praying for others, God started to raise up others to pray for me. Let me share once again a true-life story from my own personal experience.

I was in Zimbabwe at the time, and we were undergoing a serious family difficulty. Being rather discouraged, I took it one night to the Lord in prayer. "Lord, I can't carry all this, interceding for the crusades and others, when I have such problems of my own. I have sown over the years; now Father, it is time for my harvest. Would you please burden intercessors all over the world to pray for me?"

THE MORE YOU PRAY FOR OTHERS, THE MORE OTHERS WILL PRAY FOR YOU.

The very next night, I walked into the intercession hall, where the intercessors were gathering for the parallel prayer to the Reinhard Bonnke crusade. A man and his wife came up to me and said, "Suzette, at 3:00 this morning, the Lord woke us up to pray for you, and this is the Scripture that He impressed upon our hearts." After that, one after another came up to me with similar experiences. "The Lord woke me at 6:00 to pray for you and your family." "The Lord burdened me with your loved ones." God is the debtor of no man. We can never out-give God. My heart was singing with joy, as I started to reap my harvest.

In the following days and weeks, I began to receive mail from people whom I never knew, who were burdened by the Lord to pray for my situation.

Is it pride or is it selfishness to seek the Lord on your own behalf? Certainly not! We have a loving, caring heavenly Father, who is concerned about our needs and worries. I had prayed long and hard for others, and now those seeds brought home the harvest that I needed at that time—my personal harvest from intercession. What you sow, you will reap.

HEAVENLY BANK ACCOUNT

How foolish it would be for anyone to walk into a bank and try to draw interest on money that he has not already deposited there. After scanning the records carefully, the clerk behind the desk would call for the bank manager to sort out the situation. However, the only remarks he could say to you would be something like, "You cannot draw interest on money that you have not ever deposited with us."

Our lives are similar to a bank account. We can get out only what we put in. Sometimes, our prayer life revolves only around our immediate needs, whether they involve personal matters, family, or friends. But if that is all you are praying for, then something is very wrong.

The generous soul will be made rich, and he who waters will also be watered himself (Proverbs 11:25).

Let me expound here a little. A generous person—spending much time in prayer, liberal in giving, unselfish in showing love and encouraging others—will prosper and be made rich (not necessarily financially). He who refreshes others will himself be refreshed. He who pours out water will have water poured out upon himself. What a wonderful promise from God!

The lazy man will not plow because of winter; he will beg during harvest and have nothing (Proverbs 20:4).

Winter is the time for plowing, for breaking up the fallow land so that, in the words of Matthew, it becomes good ground, which will bear fruit and produce a harvest.

But he who received seed on the good ground is he who hears the word and understands it, who indeed bears fruit and produces: some a hundredfold, some sixty, some thirty (Matthew 13:23).

Harvest time is a time for gathering in that which has already been sown. It is payback time for the work already done.

As in the natural, so in the spiritual—the time to pray is now, when you have time and ability and are not beset with crises. Then, when problems and difficulties surround you, there is a fruitful harvest to be reaped.

Many are so desperately poor in their heavenly bank account because there has been little or no deposit; therefore, there is little or nothing to withdraw. Look around and start praying for others—even nations, so that others will start praying for you.

> YOU CANNOT DRAW INTEREST ON MONEY THAT YOU HAVE NOT EVER DEPOSITED.

Ask of Me, and I will give you the nations for your inheritance, and the ends of the earth for your possession (Psalm 2:8).

EQUAL SHAREHOLDERS

When you understand it correctly, the concept of being an equal shareholder in a spiritual harvest is somewhat staggering. The best way of explaining it is by yet another personal example.

I came into full-time Christian ministry only 18 months after I had been born again. And although I was a mature woman, qualified midwife, and registered nurse, I was only a beginner spiritually; but I was a beginner with a passion.

I had a real empathy with those saints who, together with their families, were suffering for the sake of the Gospel, especially behind the "Iron Curtain" at that time. I prayed for them by name; I prayed for them in their imprisonment; and I prayed for them to be strong and courageous. Sometimes the prayers were long and anguished; and at other times, they were short and simple. But I prayed for them. I did not know that this was called intercession, as I was rather inexperienced in the things of God. Even so, I prayed. What it is called is irrelevant; it is the passion that counts. Little did I know that it was the training ground God was going to use to teach me greater dimensions in intercession.

At that time, I was a member of the Reinhard Bonnke team. And one day, as I was sitting on the stage as Evangelist Bonnke was preaching the Gospel, I said, "Lord, there must be something more that I can do than just sitting on this stage."

"Yes, there is! You can start to become active in the spirit realm."

I said, "What? Lord, I don't know what You are talking about."

The Lord then began to show me what this involved, using the passage regarding Moses, Aaron, and Hur from Exodus chapter 17.

> *Now Amalek came and fought with Israel in Rephidim. And Moses said to Joshua, "Choose us some men and go out, fight with Amalek. Tomorrow I will stand on the top of the hill with the rod of God in my hand." So Joshua did as Moses said to him, and fought with Amalek. And Moses, Aaron, and Hur went up to the top of the hill. And so it was,* **when Moses held up his hand, that Israel prevailed**; *and when he let down his hand, Amalek prevailed. But Moses' hands became heavy; so they took a stone and put it under him, and he sat on it. And* **Aaron and Hur supported his hands**, *one on one side, and the other on the other side; and his hands were steady until the going down of the sun. So Joshua defeated Amalek and his people with the edge of the sword* (Exodus 17:8-13).

Here, we read that when Moses' arms were held aloft, Israel prevailed. However, when his hands dropped because of fatigue and exhaustion, the Amalekites prevailed. Aaron and Hur rose to the occasion. They sat Moses down, so that he would not tire so easily, and supported his arms. Both of them were *together with* Moses *against* the Amalekites. They stepped into the gap and helped Moses. This is the role of the intercessor.

EQUAL SHAREHOLDERS SHARE EQUALLY IN THE VICTORY OR DEFEAT OF THE BATTLE.

Without Aaron and Hur, Moses would not have been able to get through the day with his arms raised. All four human parties—Aaron, Hur, Moses, and the army of Israel—won a mighty victory that day, and the enemy was vanquished. This is the significance of "equal shareholders." We share equally in the victory or defeat of the battle.

> *Then the Lord said to Moses, "Write this for a memorial in the book and recount it in the hearing of Joshua, that **I will utterly blot out the remembrance of Amalek from under heaven***" (Exodus 17:14).

Following that lesson from the Lord, I soon learned to pray, sometimes quietly in my spirit. In whatever meeting I found myself in, I prayed for the pastor, for the preacher, for the music team. I prayed for all those taking part in the service. And as I prayed, my spirit became active, and spiritually, I held up the arms of the one ministering. As a result, I became an equal shareholder of whatever was happening in the spirit realm during that service.

This is the very reason that even now, although I have my own mission organization, I still intercede for the Reinhard Bonnke Crusades while they are taking place, no matter where I am. Why? It is so that I can be an equal shareholder in the mighty revival harvest that is taking place.

This type of prayer is also the way to affect the world situation. You do not have to be a preacher or evangelist to receive that great reward. By coming alongside a "Moses" and holding up his arms, you are an equal shareholder in the spoils of that victory. This is the intercessor's personal harvest. If more people could grasp this concept, we would not have such jealousy in the church where people feel that they have not been granted a position or a task.

FIVE FINGERS AND A HAND

Intercession works in a similar manner to your hand. Your fingers and thumb represent the fivefold ministry. Each one is peculiar to itself. The index finger is nothing like the little finger, which is different from the middle finger. However, without the palm, none of them are able to function correctly. Although they each seem to be independent, they work only through the palm of the hand. No palm—no fingers!

This represents the Church. The palm is the Body of Christ, which enables the fivefold ministry to operate efficiently. As intercession flows from the Church, various ministries carry out their function. Without that support, intercession ceases; then, as when Moses' arms fell down, victory is in jeopardy. You are the Aarons and the Hurs, who are called to support your leaders.

When the Church begins to pray with passion and intercedes for the leaders, there is no time for jealousy, as everyone is involved in the whole of the battle. We are not working for man but for God. David had a good understanding of this concept when he said:

> *For who will heed you in this matter? But as his part is who goes down to the battle, so shall his part be who stays by the supplies; they shall share alike* (1 Samuel 30:24).

Whether your role is to be on the front line in hand-to-hand combat or at the rear with the baggage train and supplies, everyone engaged in that conflict shares alike in the victory spoils. They all are equal shareholders in the booty.

Consider what Joshua had to say when he spoke with the Reubenites, Gadites, and the half tribe of Manasseh, before they went back across the Jordan to their own land. They all had fought the good fight to conquer the land, and now they were about to depart to their homes and families.

> *…Return with much riches to your tents, with very much livestock, with silver, with gold, with bronze, with iron, and with very much clothing.* **Divide the spoil of your enemies** *with your brethren* (Joshua 22:8).

Every time a soul is saved, every time a person is healed or delivered, the enemy is plundered, and the spoils are taken from him. All our spoils are in Christ Jesus, and in Him we become equal shareholders.

However, there are times when we can lose a share that we might have gained. One day, at one of the Reinhard Bonnke crusades, I had allowed myself to be seriously distracted during the meeting. Then, when the altar call was given, the Holy Spirit spoke to me, and informed me that I had earned no share in that harvest of those souls because I had not been active on their behalf. I had lost my personal harvest for that meeting because of the distraction. I promised the Lord, there and then, that that would never happen again.

> EVERY TIME A SOUL IS SAVED, EVERY TIME A PERSON IS HEALED OR DELIVERED, THE ENEMY IS PLUNDERED.

I highly appreciate good administration, but I often ask myself whether we really need to be so busy with some small detail during the meeting that we allow ourselves to be distracted from the Word of God. Of course, those types of matters are dealt with, for the Lord; and yet, if we are honest, many of those things can wait until later. Our team makes it a point to be present during the meetings, as the Word of God has utter priority, unless there is a real emergency to be dealt with. How often do you allow your spirit to be distracted, and by that, rob you from your own harvest?

THE REWARDS OF INTERCESSION

1. Intercession is dependent upon God's ability.

2. Intercession allows you to serve on the executive council of world evangelism.

   Ask of Me, and I will give you the nations for your inheritance, and the ends of the earth for your possession (Psalm 2:8).

3. Intercession allows you to pray that which is on the heart of the Father.

   Now He who searches the hearts knows what the mind of the Spirit is, because He makes intercession for the saints according to the will of God (Romans 8:27).

4. Through intercession, you become a coworker with Christ.

5. Intercession builds you up in your most holy faith.

> *But you, beloved, building yourselves up on your most holy faith, praying in the Holy Spirit* (Jude 1:20).

6. Intercession enables you to become a shareholder in what God is doing.

    > *For who will heed you in this matter? But as his part is who goes down to the battle, so shall his part be who stays by the supplies; they shall share alike* (1 Samuel 30:24).

7. Intercession brings you into the law of sowing and reaping.

    > *But this I say: He who sows sparingly will also reap sparingly, and he who sows bountifully will also reap bountifully* (2 Corinthians 9:6).

.

CHAPTER 3

_____

Spiritual Warfare—Part One

THERE ARE "EXPERTS" WHO SAY that there is no such thing as spiritual warfare, or that the subject has been taken totally out of context. Indeed, everyone has a right to their own opinion, but you might be hard-pressed to share their view by the time you have finished reading the next two chapters.

VICTORY IS SURE!

Worldwide, I often meet prayers and intercessors who are utterly exhausted, because they have fought the battle in their own strength, thinking that *they* have to win the war…an utterly wrong assumption. *The war has already been won!* It has been achieved at Calvary, when Christ died, was buried, and three days later was resurrected from the dead.

> *For to this end Christ died and rose and lived again, that He might be **Lord of both the dead and the living*** (Romans 14:9).

> *And being found in appearance as a man, He humbled Himself and became obedient to the point of death, even **the death of the cross**. Therefore God also has highly exalted Him and given Him the name which is above every name, that at the name of*

49

Jesus every knee should bow, of those in heaven, and of those on earth, and of those under the earth, and that every tongue should confess that **Jesus Christ is Lord,** *to the glory of God the Father* (Philippians 2:8-11).

He [Jesus] *died for all, that those who live should live no longer for themselves, but for Him who died for them and rose again* (2 Corinthians 5:15).

As we mentioned in the last chapter, the debtor's account has been paid in full. In Christ, we have the victory. However, we are still in a battle. Although the strategic victory has been won, the tactical battle continues.

For we do not wrestle against flesh and blood, but against principalities, against powers, against the rulers of the darkness of this age, against spiritual hosts of wickedness in the heavenly places (Ephesians 6:12).

SATAN CONTINUES THE BATTLE, EVEN THOUGH HE HAS LOST THE WAR.

With every victory, there is a battlefield. Calvary was the scene of the ultimate battle, but even so, there are still conflicts that affect our everyday life. Satan continues the battle, even though he has already lost against Christ. He continues to attack those whom Jesus has paid for and loves—you and me. For that reason, we are constantly engaged in spiritual warfare, whether we want to admit it or not.

Sir Winston Churchill's famous comment concerning the battle of El Alamein is interesting in this respect. "Before Alamein we never had a victory; after Alamein we never had a defeat." Likewise, in the spirit realm, before Calvary, we never had a victory; after Calvary, we never had a defeat. The battle rages, but the glorious army of the Lord Jesus Christ moves from victory to victory. Of course, there are setbacks, trials, and tribulations; nevertheless, the war has been won, and total victory is assured.

Child of God, it is not your job to win that victory; rather, it is your job as well as mine to reinforce, to proclaim, to preach, to declare, and to confess the triumphant victory that Christ has won for us already! And along with that, to possess, claim back, and hold the ground gained and won through Calvary.

I often compare the attacks of the enemy to guerrilla warfare in which members of an irregular armed force fight a stronger force by sabotage and harassment. The purpose of such guerrilla warfare is to destroy communications and unity and to try to enforce fear and confusion. With these tactics, satan and his forces continue to attack the children of God. Contrarily, by reinforcing, proclaiming, praying God's Word, standing on the promises of God, and worship, we have total victory over these guerrilla tactics.

> WE DO NOT WIN THE VICTORY; WE PROCLAIM THE VICTORY.

In the Bible, several characters exhibited this attitude of noncompliance to enemy demands. Think about Joshua and Caleb and their reaction and opinion to the dismal report of the ten other spies:

> *Then Caleb quieted the people before Moses, and said, "Let us go up at once and take possession, for we are well able to overcome it"* (Numbers 13:30).

No matter how strong or fearsome the enemy is, with God on the side of the righteous, there can only be victory. Had the Israelites gone into the Promised Land at the promptings of Joshua and Caleb, there would certainly have been many fierce and prolonged battles, as there were when they went in 40 years later. Nevertheless, in spite of many being killed or maimed in the conflicts, the overall victory was assured.

> *The Lord your God will expel them from before you and drive them out of your sight. So **you shall possess their land, as the Lord your God promised you*** (Joshua 23:5).

Many more examples can be mentioned here, including David (see 1 Sam. 17:45), Ezra (see Ezra 8:21-23), and not to mention the chapter of the "heroes" (see Heb. 11). When the enemy sought to impose his rules and restrictions, the servants of God fought against him with everything that they had, up to and including their lives if necessary.

TRIUMPHANT ONLY IN CHRIST

When satan took over our land in the Garden of Eden, he caused Eve to partake of the fruit; Adam followed suit.

> *So the Lord God said to the serpent: "Because you have done this, you are cursed more than all cattle, and more than every beast of*

the field; on your belly you shall go, and you shall eat dust all the days of your life. And I will put enmity between you and the woman, and between your seed and her Seed; He shall bruise your head, and you shall bruise His heel" (Genesis 3:14-15).

The world waged a guerrilla war with the seed of satan, until Christ came, and then the roles were reversed. The battle belongs to the Lord, and the forces of darkness are now carrying out *their* guerrilla war against the children of God.

Now to Abraham and his Seed were the promises made. He does not say, "And to seeds," as of many, but as of one, "and to your Seed," who is Christ (Galatians 3:16).

If we attempt to fight the enemy in our own strength, then we will fall victim to some well-planned enemy attack.

You and I are no match for satan. He is the fallen cherub, probably the mightiest creature that God has ever created, although still a creature and subservient to Almighty God. In any case, you and I are not capable in our human ability—no matter how powerful we think we are. But thankfully, in Christ, we fight *together with* Him and *against* the enemy. When we do it in that order—in Christ, *together with against*—the enemy has to run (see James 4:7).

Now thanks be to God who always leads us in triumph in Christ, and through us diffuses the fragrance of His knowledge in every place. For we are to God the fragrance of Christ among those who are being saved and among those who are perishing (2 Corinthians 2:14-15).

OUR MANDATE—PROCLAIM THE MANIFOLD WISDOM OF GOD

Christ has given us all the equipment necessary to enforce the triumphant victory that He has already won. We are His "ambassadors of the cross," and it is as such that our mandate for spiritual warfare lies. The mandate is written for us to study and apply. Paul wrote it to the Ephesians:

To me, who am less than the least of all the saints, this grace was given, that I should preach among the Gentiles the unsearchable *riches of Christ, and to make all see what is the fellowship of the mystery, which from the beginning of the ages has been hidden in God who created all things through Jesus Christ; to the intent that now **the manifold wisdom of God might be made known by the church to the principalities and powers in the heavenly places**, according to the eternal purpose which He accomplished in Christ Jesus our Lord, in whom we have boldness and access with confidence through faith in Him* (Ephesians 3:8-12).

As ambassadors of the cross, it is our duty to proclaim to the principalities and powers in heavenly places the manifold wisdom of God. We, as the Body of Christ, are to show forth and display the power of God to the forces of darkness.

So what is this "manifold wisdom of God"? What does it mean? The word *manifold* simply means "many and varied; having many features or forms," and such is the wisdom of God, which is described in the Scripture above as the "unsearchable riches of Christ."

When the Word of God is preached, the manifold wisdom is imparted.

When somebody is set free, the manifold wisdom of God is displayed.

When a miracle happens, it is the manifold wisdom of God in action.

When we pray and God answers our prayer, the manifold wisdom of God is manifested.

This manifold wisdom incorporates far more than just preaching the Gospel, healing, or delivering someone; it is the whole revealed expression of the Word. And it is not limited to one or two popularized events. As ambassadors of the cross, our mandate is to present the *full* Gospel—not just parts of it, and not just the parts that fit our own personal understanding and theology.

Every time that we move by the grace and mercy of the Lord in any of these wonderful gifts with which He has endowed us, then the manifold wisdom of God is displayed in all its heavenly glory to the powers of darkness. That is spiritual warfare!

Just to drive in that nail of understanding, let me repeat for the sake of clarity that the only foundation on which to address the

OUR MANDATE IS TO PRESENT THE FULL GOSPEL—NOT JUST PARTS OF IT.

forces of darkness, or even to exercise any authority in the name of Jesus, is the cross and the cross alone. That which happened on the cross of Jesus Christ is our only strength and basis for spiritual warfare.

Satan fears the name of Jesus Christ. He fears the power of the cross, because it was on the cross that Christ's divine blood was shed, which stripped him (satan) of all his power. It was the appointed time and place for satan's head to be bruised.

> *And according to the law almost all things are purified with blood, and **without shedding of blood there is no remission*** (Hebrews 9:22).

> *Much more then, **having now been justified by His blood**, we shall be saved from wrath through Him* (Romans 5:9).

> *In this is love, not that we loved God, but that He loved us and sent His Son to be **the propitiation for our sins*** (1 John 4:10).

> *And I will put enmity between you and the woman, and between your seed and her Seed; **He shall bruise your head**, and you shall bruise His heel* (Genesis 3:15).

Unto us has been given the name of Christ, and that name represents all He was, is, and ever will be. All power and authority is wrapped up in this name.

> *Let it be known to you all, and to all the people of Israel, that by **the name of Jesus Christ of Nazareth**, whom you crucified, whom God raised from the dead, by Him this man stands here before you whole. This is the "stone which was rejected by you builders, which has become the chief cornerstone." Nor is there salvation in any other, for there is **no other name under heaven given among men by which we must be saved*** (Acts 4:10-12).

Another powerful verse that shows the totality of satan's defeat is:

> *And you, being dead in your trespasses and the uncircumcision of your flesh, He has made alive together with Him, having forgiven you all trespasses, having wiped out the handwriting of requirements that was against us, which was contrary to us. And He has taken it out of the way, having nailed it to the cross. Having **disarmed principalities and powers**, He made a public spectacle of them, triumphing over them in it* (Colossians 2:13-15).

Having established our mandate, there are two subjects to address before moving on—*fear* and *worship*.

FEAR

Fear is one of the most powerful tools that satan uses to prevent God's people from exercising their authority in spiritual warfare. Yet the only one who should be afraid is satan. We are not to fear. Many times, Jesus said to people, "Fear not." You do not have to worry that when you engage in spiritual warfare, all manner of problems will beset you, your family, or your church. God's Word clearly states:

If God is for us, who can be against us? (Romans 8:31b)

You are never on your own against the enemy. The writer to the Hebrews puts it this way:

For He Himself has said, "I will never leave you nor forsake you" (Hebrews 13:5c).

If you abide in the Vine, then there is absolutely no reason why you should ever come into any fear. If you walk in Christ Jesus your Lord, according to the Spirit, then fear should never be a part of your vocabulary. Never let fear hold you back!

Abide in Me, and I in you. As the branch cannot bear fruit of itself, unless it abides in the vine, neither can you, unless you abide in Me (John 15:4).

*As you therefore have received Christ Jesus the Lord, so **walk in Him*** (Colossians 2:6).

Fear is as powerful as faith, but in reverse. Faith is the substance that pleases God, and fear is the substance that pleases satan.

Now faith is the substance of things hoped for, the evidence of things not seen (Hebrews 11:1).

But without faith it is impossible to please Him, for he who comes to God must believe that He is, and that He is a rewarder of those who diligently seek Him (Hebrews 11:6).

Fear and faith are powerful forces that work in opposite directions. It is impossible to be neutral when we move in faith, as faith is always active and moving forward. Whereas, fear limits, prevents action, and brings forth bondage. Allowing fear in your life is to say to God, "You are not able to handle this situation."

WORSHIP

Worship and an upright life before God are your protection. I find it vital to get back into worship after a time of spiritual warfare, to refocus my mind totally on God. Worship refreshes and builds your spirit again. However, that all depends upon what is considered as worship.

WORSHIP IS THE EXPRESSION OF YOUR LOVE BEFORE ALMIGHTY GOD.

Worship is not three fast songs followed by two slow ones, in order to work up the right atmosphere.

Worship is the expression of your love before Him. It can be loud or soft. It might be by song, but it does not necessarily have to be. You can be in silent adoration without ever opening your mouth, and yet be in the deepest worship. (More about worship is found in Chapter 9—"The Song of the Lord.")

It is more important to worship than to go to war! You are not redeemed and saved to make war; you are redeemed and saved to glorify Almighty God. You are saved to have fellowship with Him.

> *God is faithful, by whom **you were called into the fellowship of His Son, Jesus Christ our Lord*** (1 Corinthians 1:9).

> *Therefore if there is any consolation in Christ, if any comfort of love, if any **fellowship of the Spirit**, if any affection and mercy* (Philippians 2:1).

> *That which we have seen and heard we declare to you, that you also may have fellowship with us; and truly **our fellowship is with the Father and with His Son Jesus Christ*** (1 John 1:3).

Christ came to this earth, not because He wanted you to fight the devil on His behalf (He has already done that single-handedly); He came to this earth because He loves you, paid a price for you, cares for you, knows your inner thoughts, your very soul, your mind. He knows everything about you. He knows your past, your present, and your future. He knows when you were in your mother's womb. He knows where you are today, and He knows where He wants to lead you tomorrow. He came to this earth because He loves you.

> *Blessed be the God and Father of our Lord Jesus Christ, who has **blessed us** with every spiritual blessing in the heavenly places in Christ, just as He **chose us** in Him before the foundation of the world, that we should be holy and without blame before Him in love, having **predestined us** to adoption as sons by Jesus Christ to Himself, according to the good pleasure of His will, to the praise of the glory of His grace, by which He **made us accepted** in the Beloved* (Ephesians 1:3-6).

When you engage in spiritual warfare, it is to reinforce what has already been accomplished. However, spiritual warfare is not the main purpose of our life. Our true purpose in this life as well as that in the next is written above—we should be holy and without blame before Him in love.

WE MUST OPEN THE DOORS FOR THE GOSPEL TO SPREAD

The ultimate goal of spiritual warfare is clearly expressed by Paul in his request to the Colossians for prayer.

> *Continue earnestly in prayer, being vigilant in it with thanksgiving; meanwhile praying also for us, that **God would open to us a door for the word, to speak the mystery of Christ**, for which I am also in chains, that I may make it manifest, as I ought to speak* (Colossians 4:2-4).

As I have stated before, the purpose of spiritual warfare is so that the Gospel of Christ can be preached and the manifold wisdom of God can be made manifest.

Many countries will not allow the preaching of the Gospel and actively suppress all Christian witness. Consequently, we have the purpose of spiritual warfare—so that those who are born again and have been given the weapons in Christ Jesus can rise up and put them to effective use, causing the doors to open so that the truth of the Gospel is made manifest to all.

Personally, I feel that so much of our spiritual warfare effort in First World countries, in which there is no persecution, has moved away from the original goal. Instead of warring in the spirit, so that the Word of God stays in our schools, or that our young people are affected by the Gospel in our universities, we concentrate on carrying out spiritual warfare against things that have nothing to do with souls.

There is also a secondary, yet similar purpose to spiritual warfare, which is *praying for those in authority* so that the Gospel can be preached openly in the land.

> *Therefore I exhort first of all that supplications, prayers, intercessions, and giving of thanks be made for all men, **for kings and all who are in authority, that we may lead a quiet and peaceable life in all godliness and reverence**. For this is good and acceptable in the sight of God our Savior, who desires all men to be saved and to come to the knowledge of the truth* (1 Timothy 2:1-4).

When is an acceptable time of salvation? Now! And if that is so, then when is an acceptable time for spiritual warfare?

> *For He says: "In an acceptable time I have heard you, and in the day of salvation I have helped you." Behold, **now is the accepted time**; behold, **now is the day of salvation*** (2 Corinthians 6:2).

THE WORD IS YOUR WEAPON

How do we engage in spiritual warfare? There are physical acts that enable spiritual warfare to be waged. As always, this involves a balanced approach. A means that is used in one particular conflict might not necessarily be used in future engagements. Just remember that satan has no creative power, so he cannot come up with new tactics. For that very reason, it is possible to know and to recognize his plans and scheming. All that we need has been given to us already in the Word.

The Bible is the ultimate weapon, for it is everlasting.

> *Heaven and earth will pass away, but My words will by no means pass away* (Luke 21:33).

Experience is a wonderful thing, but we cannot build foundations upon experience. It is like building a house on sand. It is supported for a while, but suddenly…

The rain descended, the floods came, and the winds blew and beat on that house; and it fell. And great was its fall (Matthew 7:27).

If your spiritual warfare is Word-based, your foundations are secure. For it is from the Word of God that the following means of warfare are taken.

1. Praise and worship.

    *Let the **high praises** of God be in their mouth, and a two-edged sword in their hand* (Psalm 149:6).

    *And when he had consulted with the people, he appointed those who should sing to the Lord, and who should **praise** the beauty of holiness, as they went out before the army and were saying: "**Praise** the Lord, for His mercy endures forever." Now when they began to sing and to **praise**, the Lord set ambushes against the people of Ammon, Moab, and Mount Seir, who had come against Judah; and they were defeated* (2 Chronicles 20:21-22).

2. Dance.

    *Let them praise His name with the **dance**; let them sing praises to Him with the timbrel and harp* (Psalm 149:3).

    *Then Miriam the prophetess, the sister of Aaron, took the timbrel in her hand; and all the women went out after her with timbrels and with **dances*** (Exodus 15:20).

3. Groaning.

    *Not only that, but we also who have the firstfruits of the Spirit, even we ourselves **groan** within ourselves, eagerly waiting for the adoption, the redemption of our body* (Romans 8:23).

    *Likewise the Spirit also helps in our weaknesses. For we do not know what we should pray for as we ought, but the Spirit Himself makes intercession for us with **groanings** which cannot be uttered* (Romans 8:26).

    *For we who are in this tent **groan**, being burdened, not because we want to be unclothed, but further clothed, that mortality may be swallowed up by life* (2 Corinthians 5:4).

4. Weeping.

> *"Now, therefore," says the Lord, "Turn to Me with all your heart, with fasting, with **weeping**, and with mourning"* (Joel 2:12).

> *Now while Ezra was praying, and while he was confessing, **weeping**, and bowing down before the house of God, a very large assembly of men, women, and children gathered to him from Israel; for the people wept very bitterly* (Ezra 10:1).

> *Who, in the days of His flesh, when He had offered up prayers and supplications, with **vehement cries and tears** to Him who was able to save Him from death, and was heard because of His godly fear* (Hebrews 5:7).

5. Shouting.

> *Now Joshua had commanded the people, saying, "You shall not **shout** or make any noise with your voice, nor shall a word proceed out of your mouth, until the day I say to you, 'Shout!' Then you shall **shout"*** (Joshua 6:10).

> *Oh come, let us sing to the Lord!* (Psalm 95:1a).

Let us *shout* joyfully to the Rock of our salvation.

> *The great day of the Lord is near; it is near and hastens quickly. The noise of the day of the Lord is bitter; there the mighty men shall **cry out*** (Zephaniah 1:14).

6. The Armor of God.

The whole armor of God is in reality the Lord Jesus Christ! In Him, we live, and move, and have our being. I personally do not believe that you need to put on the armor every day. But my question is: Do you have the armor available when you need it? The armor of God is there to apply when the attack of the enemy comes. For example, apply your faith in times of crises (your shield); apply the truth of the Word (your girdle); etc. That is what Ephesians chapter 6 implies.

PROPHETIC INTERCESSION

Prophetic intercession and acts are very controversial. Nevertheless, if in doubt, check it out! No matter who has brought the teaching, if you are in any doubt about the matter, go to the very source of problem-solving—the Word of God. Study it; spend time in prayer before the Lord so that the Spirit of God can lead you into all truth.

> *However, when He, the Spirit of truth, has come,* **He will guide you into all truth***; for He will not speak on His own authority, but whatever He hears He will speak; and He will tell you things to come* (John 16:13).

A good biblical example of prophetic intercession is one that we have used previously to illustrate the concept of *together with against*— Moses, Aaron, and Hur.

> *So Joshua did as Moses said to him, and fought with Amalek. And Moses, Aaron, and Hur went up to the top of the hill. And so it was, when Moses held up his hand, that Israel prevailed; and when he let down his hand, Amalek prevailed* (Exodus 17:10-11).

While Moses held aloft the rod of God, Israel was victorious; yet when his arms drooped, Amalek prevailed. Moses' arms and rod were a symbol of his intercession before God. In the natural, an 80-year-old man with a piece of wood in his hand was no match for a fit, young Amalekite warrior. There would have been no contest. However, it was in the spiritual realm that this symbolic gesture was having its greatest effect.

The Spirit of the Lord might lead you to perform some action that of itself is quite meaningless but in the spiritual realm may be like a nuclear explosion!

Another example, which involved Joshua and an apparently meaningless gesture, is as follows:

> *Then the Lord said to Joshua, "Stretch out the spear that is in your hand toward Ai, for I will give it into your hand." And Joshua stretched out the spear that was in his hand toward the city* (Joshua 8:18).

Joshua exhibited great faith in Jehovah, as he pointed a spear toward the city, in full anticipation of a victory.

If the Lord impresses upon you prophetic intercession, the actions will probably be quite simple yet meaningful, but only within the context of a specific situation. We never again read of Moses ever holding his arms aloft during a battle, nor do we discover that Joshua was ever again directed to point a spear at another city.

PROPHETIC INTERCESSION AND ACTS ARE FOR A SPECIFIC SITUATION.

Do not make your prophetic intercession or act a religious symbol that must be invoked, replayed, or reenacted again and again. It will not work. Prophetic intercession and acts are for a specific situation given by God to be exercised at that specific time in order to produce a specific result. It is not to be made the next doctrine. Beware of going out of balance by putting more emphasis on the prophetic act than on the simple praying of the Word of God itself. Be free in Christ—do what He lays on your heart to do, but do not expect everybody else to do the same or to follow your example. He gave it to you—and only you—to do.

CHAPTER 4

Spiritual Warfare—Part Two

IN THE LAST CHAPTER, WE concentrated on the biblical foundation of spiritual warfare; whereas, in this chapter, we will consider the practical aspects of that warfare.

As was mentioned earlier, every victory has its own battlefield. Every conflict must be fought over some territory. The ideal territory for a tank battle is not a mountainous region with deep valleys and ravines. Instead, that is excellent guerrilla territory. To use tanks, the ideal terrain is the open countryside, vast rolling plains, flatlands, where from horizon to horizon all that can be seen is waving grass and undulating hillocks. Likewise, we must understand and realize the ideal elements for our spiritual battlefield.

SATAN'S BATTLEFIELD—THE MIND

First, let's consider where the enemy is most likely to attack. What is the ideal battlefield for satan to mount his guerrilla attacks upon the child of God? It is the human mind! Satan battles for the focus of your mind, and his ultimate plan is to divert that focus away from God and onto yourself, to divert your mind off the Creator and onto the creation.

Although satan has no creative power, he still remains a very powerful spirit, yet limited in his abilities. Satan is not a creator; therefore, he has to exist with what he has been given. He cannot create new ideas, new plans, new scenarios; he has to make the best use of what he has—and he definitely knows how to put his limited resources to good use.

SATAN IS NOT A CREATOR; THEREFORE, HE HAS TO EXIST WITH WHAT HE HAS BEEN GIVEN.

When satan tells you that you are not good enough, or that you are not capable, he is actually speaking the truth. Man in his own right is not good enough. However, wearing the robe of righteousness and clothed in the garment of praise, then in Christ, we are good enough; we are more than conquerors.

I can do all things through Christ who strengthens me (Philippians 4:13).

Child of God, the only time that you will be perfect is when you are in glory with the Lord Jesus Christ. Until then, it is not our goodness or righteousness that counts; it is the blood of Jesus that makes us worthy to stand before His throne.

Every time that satan whispers these human truths about your abilities, and you listen to them and accept them, he is able to hamper the overall victory through his guerrilla maneuvers. Sabotage and harassment are his constant tactics to wear down the child of God who has not understood the significance of spiritual warfare.

The Word of God emphasizes how important the mind is:

*And do not be conformed to this world, but be transformed by **the renewing of your mind**, that you may prove what is that good and acceptable and perfect will of God* (Romans 12:2).

*Put off, concerning your former conduct, the old man which grows corrupt according to the deceitful lusts, and **be renewed in the spirit of your mind**, and that you put on the new man which was created according to God, in true righteousness and holiness* (Ephesians 4:22-24).

Here, we have an understanding of satan's main battlefield—the human mind! In the Strong's Concordance, the word *mind* comes from the Greek "dianoia," which suggests understanding, insight, meditation, reflection, perception, the faculty of thought. The human mind is like a sponge. A sponge soaks up any type of liquid, water, petrol, or acid. If it is dropped into liquid sewage, it absorbs it with no problem. If the human mind is soaked in the filth of debauchery, it absorbs it just as easily. So knowing what the human mind is like, satan aims to direct it away from God and onto the satisfying of one's self. Paul tells us quite clearly, what we should do:

> *Finally, brethren, whatever things are true, whatever things are noble, whatever things are just, whatever things are pure, whatever things are lovely, whatever things are of good report, if there is any virtue and if there is anything praiseworthy—meditate on these things* (Philippians 4:8).

Consider how satan inveigled his way into the minds of the Israelites following the exodus out of Egypt. The Israelites had been rescued from abysmal slavery; the sea opened before them; they escaped from the pursuing Egyptian forces; and they saw the cloud by day and the column of fire by night that directed them on their journey. At Mount Horeb, where the mountain burned with fire to the midst of Heaven, with darkness, cloud, and thick darkness, the Lord spoke to them. Every day, they collected their daily rations fresh from the ground; water came out of a rock to refresh them. If ever a young nation was focused upon Almighty God, it was the nation of Israel.

Yet somehow, satan managed to get in amongst them and redirect their focus away from God and onto themselves. It is the oldest trick in his armory, and it is quite effective. Eve felt the force of this subtle refocusing when the serpent said, "Has God indeed said…?" As a result, Eve was deceived, and we all know the result.

> *So when the woman saw that the tree was good for food, that it was pleasant to the eyes, and a tree desirable to make one wise, she took of its fruit and ate. She also gave to her husband with her, and he ate* (Genesis 3:6).

But that was just one woman. Indeed, how could satan come up with a strategy that would sway a whole nation? He did it in exactly the same way! He influenced ten of the twelve spies.

The Lord sent out the 12; they spied out the land and returned with a report for Moses. The first part of the report was encouraging—they described the land as flowing with milk and honey.

> *We went to the land where you sent us. It truly flows with milk and honey, and this is its fruit* (Numbers 13:27b).

If they had stopped there, everything would have been fine. The Israelites would have entered the land as a victorious, conquering army. However, satan had been at work in their minds, as the latter part of their report revealed:

> *Nevertheless the people who dwell in the land are strong; the cities are fortified and very large; moreover we saw the descendants of Anak there. The Amalekites dwell in the land of the South; the Hittites, the Jebusites, and the Amorites dwell in the mountains; and the Canaanites dwell by the sea and along the banks of the Jordan* (Numbers 13:28-29).

They took their eyes off Jehovah, and looked to themselves. Even after an encouraging speech from Caleb, they could only look to themselves.

> *But the men who had gone up with him said, "We are not able to go up against the people, for they are stronger than we." And they gave the children of Israel a bad report of the land which they had spied out, saying, "The land through which we have gone as spies is a land that devours its inhabitants, and all the people whom we saw in it are men of great stature. There we saw the giants (the descendants of Anak came from the giants); and* **we were like grasshoppers in our own sight,** *and so we were in their sight"* (Numbers 13:31-33).

"We were like grasshoppers in our own sight"—satan's refocusing had worked! Had their eyes been fixed upon the living God and His ability, they would have been undefeatable. In the words of an old hymn:

> *Turn your eyes upon Jesus,*
> *Look full in His wonderful face.*
> *And the things of earth will grow strangely dim,*
> *In the light of His glory and grace.* [1]

Peter had an antidote to this refocusing tactic of the enemy.

*Therefore **gird up the loins of your mind**, be sober, and rest your hope fully upon the grace that is to be brought to you at the revelation of Jesus Christ* (1 Peter 1:13).

The responsibility of this "girding up" lies with each individual. In fact, the literal translation of this passage is: "having girded up the loins of your mind." Then you can go on to be sober, and rest upon the grace. This is a metaphor derived from the practice of the Orientals, who in order to be unimpeded in their movements, were accustomed, when starting a journey or engaging in any work, to bind their long flowing garments closely around their bodies and fasten them with a leather belt.

Attack by Way of the Senses

Satan's tactic is to impede the movements of a previously unfettered mind. Now, when you understand that satan's ultimate battlefield is the mind, then you are already in a victorious position over the enemy. However, how does he actually manage to refocus our mind?

It is really quite simple—he works through our senses.

*For all that is in the world—**the lust of the flesh, the lust of the eyes, and the pride of life**—is not of the Father but is of the world* (1 John 2:16).

Jesus said,

What comes out of a man, that defiles a man. For from within, out of the heart of men, proceed evil thoughts, adulteries, fornications, murders, thefts, covetousness, wickedness, deceit, lewdness, an evil eye, blasphemy, pride, foolishness. All these evil things come from within and defile a man (Mark 7:20-23).

The Bible says that "faith comes by hearing and hearing by the word of God," which also happens to be the way that unbelief comes—by hearing. Let me paraphrase—unbelief comes by hearing and hearing by the negative things spoken to your spirit.

Satan works through the hearing, and he works by what you see. It is no wonder that Job says:

I have made a covenant with my eyes; why then should I look upon a young woman? (Job 31:1)

Job knew that what he allowed himself to see would affect his spirit. It is the same with you. Whatever you allow your eyes to look upon and to see will affect your spirit. That which is in the heart, eventually comes out, just as the Lord Jesus said. I always maintain:

> *You are tomorrow what you say today;*
> *and you will be today what you said yesterday.*

This is the battlefield. It is where satan tries to influence you, by bringing depression or limitation. He tries to get your eyes upon yourself, your ability, and who you are. Whereas, when the mind is renewed by the Holy Spirit, the entire mind-set changes from a timid, fearful, and negative thought-life (which is the carnal mind) to a vibrant, positive, confident thinking of the quickened spiritual mind.

PERFECT PEACE

Another result of renewing your mind in the spirit is peace.

> *You will keep him in **perfect peace**, whose mind is stayed on You, because he trusts in You* (Isaiah 26:3).

This is an incredible promise of peace; but, as in many biblical promises, there is a condition attached—"whose mind is stayed on You"—on the Creator, not the creation.

This promise does not guarantee an untroubled and blissful time. There is no declaration of peace signed with the enemy in this promise—rather the opposite. The Lord Jesus said to His disciples:

> *Peace I leave with you, My peace I give to you; not as the world gives do I give to you. Let not your heart be troubled, neither let it be afraid* (John 14:27).

Two chapters later, the Lord repeats His promise, with further explanation:

> *These things I have spoken to you, that in Me you may have peace. **In the world you will have tribulation**; but be of good cheer, I have overcome the world* (John 16:33).

We are guaranteed trouble; however, we are also guaranteed peace!

A disciple is not above his teacher, nor a servant above his master. It is enough for a disciple that he be like his teacher, and a servant like his master. If they have called the master of the house Beelzebub, how much more will they call those of his household! Therefore do not fear them (Matthew 10:24-26a).

Isaiah talks about perfect peace for the one whose mind is stayed upon the Lord. Why is this? It is because the Lord is the Prince of peace, and He indwells you.

For unto us a Child is born, unto us a Son is given; and the government will be upon His shoulder. And His name will be called Wonderful, Counselor, Mighty God, Everlasting Father, **Prince of Peace** (Isaiah 9:6).

But if the Spirit of Him who raised Jesus from the dead **dwells in you**, *He who raised Christ from the dead will also give life to your mortal bodies through* **His Spirit who dwells in you** (Romans 8:11).

*And what agreement has the temple of God with idols? For you are the temple of the living God. As God has said: "***I will dwell in them** *and walk among them. I will be their God, and they shall be My people"* (2 Corinthians 6:16).

Thus, there is peace for the believer, whose mind is focused upon the Lord and not upon the world; and it is against this peace that satan directs his guerrilla tactics. Now, satan cannot attack the eternal gift of salvation that belongs to each child of God, which has been secured in the Lord Jesus Christ; but he can attack the repository of the gift, which is the mind.

COUNTERATTACK—HUMBLE AND SUBMIT YOURSELF TO GOD WHILE RESISTING THE DEVIL

What can we do about all these attacks through which the enemy daily harasses and impedes us? The Holy Spirit did not leave us to work out a strategy all on our own. He has provided the overall blueprint for a successful counterattack.

Almighty God has provided an inexhaustible supply of munitions for us to use in the counterattack.

He gives more grace. Therefore He says: "God resists the proud, but gives grace to the humble" (James 4:6).

Grace is Heaven's secret weapon. The world has no understanding of the power of grace; indeed, it has no understanding of grace, period. These additional resources of grace enable the believer to overcome the love of the world and all its allurements. God gives grace and strength to the humble but sets Himself against the proud and haughty.

Therefore humble yourselves under the mighty hand of God, that He may exalt you in due time, casting all your care upon Him, for He cares for you (1 Peter 5:6-7).

What is humility? Humility is an attitude of heart—not what we do, or do not do, in the physical. I know many people who are soft and sweet and yet have tremendous rebellion in their hearts, or others who are strong with a lot of charisma yet they are totally humble of spirit. It is how we act in the presence of God, and with one another, that portrays the true attitude of humility.

~

WORSHIP IS THE BEST MEDICINE AGAINST PRIDE!

~

How do we humble ourselves? The best way is through worship. Worship is the best medicine against pride! The more you worship in spirit and truth, the more the Holy Spirit can reveal to you. The more you worship, the more the Holy Spirit can bring revelation to you of who He is. What is the only faculty over which you have control? It is your own will. You and you alone determine how and when you will worship. God is a gentleman; He forces no one. And for that very reason, nobody will be kidnapped into Heaven. The decision always belongs to us.

Let me remind you of what was mentioned in the previous chapter: *Worship is the expression of your love, not a song that you sing.* Sometimes, after a time of intense prayer, I feel truly exhausted. However, I have learned the wonderful secret of becoming totally quiet before the Lord. I do not pray, I do not sing, I do not talk; rather, I allow my spirit to be ministered to by some gentle worship music. This is one of my own secrets in maintaining my balance in God.

Having humbled yourself, the next instruction is to submit to God. This is most important.

Therefore submit to God (James 4:7a).

Submit, or put yourself under the command of the Lord of hosts. This does not mean that you have to be perfect, but it does mean that you have to be born again, as it is only in true salvation that there is protection! This ability to resist the devil has nothing to do with maturity; it is simply dependency on the Lord and the power of His Word. This means that the youngest and the oldest Christian can resist the enemy; consequently, he has to obey them both equally.

It is important at this point to read what the Word of God says. "Resist." It does not say, "Talk to, hold a conversation with, shout at, rebuke," or anything else. It simply says, "Resist."

A dictionary definition of *resist* is: "Stand up or offer resistance to somebody or something. Refuse to comply."

What is difficult to understand in those simple definitions? Refuse to comply with the refocusing tactics of satan, and you are resisting. We are told to resist the devil, not to bind him in chains and cast him into the lake of fire or any other esoteric actions.

After a time of strong prayer in spiritual warfare, or in resisting the enemy, it is time to draw back into that safe haven of the Lord through worship, in order to refresh and strengthen your spirit through the reading of the Word, which is a lamp to your feet and a light to your path (see Ps. 119:105).

THE ARMOR OF GOD

Put on the whole armor of God, that you may be able to stand against the wiles of the devil. For we do not wrestle against flesh and blood, but against principalities, against powers, against the rulers of the darkness of this age, against spiritual hosts of wickedness in the heavenly places. Therefore take up the whole armor of God, that you may be able to withstand in the evil day, and having done all, to stand. Stand therefore, having girded your waist with truth, having put on the breastplate of righteousness, and having shod your feet with the preparation of the gospel of peace; above all, taking the shield of faith with which you will be able to quench all the fiery darts of the wicked one. And take the helmet of salvation, and the sword of the Spirit, which is the word of God (Ephesians 6:11-17).

No matter what you see when you look into a mirror, that is not what the devil sees. Satan is spirit, so he sees in spirit. He sees a formidable warrior standing before him, armed from head to toe in heavenly armor. He looks you up and down, and what does he see?

He sees the helmet of salvation; the breastplate of righteousness; the girdle of truth; your feet shod with the preparation of the Gospel; and there, right in his face, he sees the shield of faith. But what he keeps backing away from is the terrifying sword of the Spirit, the Word of God. That is the devil's perspective of your Monday morning look in the mirror.

You are his enemy, and somehow, he has to overcome that impenetrable armor. But how is he going to do it, and what does he have with which to do it?

A quick look at his resources reveals that he has so little upon which to rely that any other normal person in his place would capitulate, sign a peace treaty, and go home to recover from the defeat—but not satan. He is such an egoist that he believes he can eventually win the battle.

*And you, being dead in your trespasses and the uncircumcision of your flesh, He has made alive together with Him, having forgiven you all trespasses, having wiped out the handwriting of requirements that was against us, which was contrary to us. And He has taken it out of the way, having nailed it to the cross. Having **disarmed principalities and powers**, He made a public spectacle of them, triumphing over them in it* (Colossians 2:13-15).

So what does he have? The Bible tells us that satan is the father of lies, but you *have the girdle of truth.*

*You are of your father the devil, and the desires of your father you want to do. He was a murderer from the beginning, and does not stand in the truth, because there is no truth in him. When he speaks a lie, he speaks from his own resources, for **he is a liar and the father of it*** (John 8:44).

He is darkness, but you *are the light of the world.*

You are the light of the world. *A city that is set on a hill cannot be hidden* (Matthew 5:14).

You *have the Word of God.* The devil has fiery darts.

*Above all, taking the shield of faith with which you will be able to quench **all the fiery darts** of the wicked one* (Ephesians 6:16).

Against his fiery darts, you *have the shield of faith.*

You are so well protected that he needs to find a different way of penetrating your defenses. Be cautioned that he can find one way in! The only means of access is through one entry point over which you stand guard—your soul! It is your mind, your will, your emotions, and your heart (not the physical pump, but the *inner you*). If he can gain access into these areas, he can begin to wreak havoc.

How does he manage to gain entry into such a well-guarded property? Well, it is not by a major frontal attack, though that can occasionally work. Usually, it is by a flanking movement, coming in unobserved from the side. He takes what you hear, what you see, what you say, what you think, and prompts you with his devilish ideas. The human heart is so evil that it turns the insignificant into serious breaches in your defense.

The heart is deceitful above all things, and desperately wicked; who can know it? (Jeremiah 17:9)

We all understand how a scratch on the skin can fester when germs get into it. This is exactly what happens in your heart. The germs of evil enter the heart, and unless the disinfectant of the Word of God is applied, it festers and causes serious problems.

*But each one is tempted when he is drawn away by his own desires and enticed. Then, **when desire has conceived, it gives birth to sin; and sin, when it is full-grown, brings forth death*** (James 1:14-15).

The fiery dart has done its work, and a conflagration has broken out. The devil knows many ways of penetrating the outer perimeter fence, and unless caught and ejected at that point, he can then advance and enlarge his territory.

As soon as that wicked word, that impure thought, or those feelings of inadequacy come, the shield of faith should be up to deflect this dart, and the sword of the Spirit should cut the evil off at its roots. This can only be maintained, however, by the renewing of your minds through the Word of God.

Is it amazing how often Christians are on the *defense* instead of the *offense*? I believe everyone should speak honestly, but I must admit that I get so tired of hearing "Oh, I'm under this attack," or "The devil is attacking me and my family in this or in that," or even "I can't seem to break through because the devil is attacking me." Let me make one thing clear—the devil has only as much power over you as you have assigned to him. That does not mean to say that we do not sometimes go through tough times, but your life as well as mine are in the hands of the living God, not in some ploy of satan. I would be as bold to say here that what we give credit to as attacks of satan are nothing else than God dealing with our flesh.

Consider two scenarios. The first is Buckingham Palace and the palace guards. There the guards stand, in full dress uniform, with whitened belts, white gloves, each with his rifle shouldered. The creases in the uniforms are razor sharp, and the boots are highly polished. They march back and forth in true soldierly manner, changing the guard, along with other duties.

The second scenario involves the same men but this time in a combat training exercise. The highly pressed and polished uniforms have been exchanged for combat clothing. There is no shine or gleam from any part of the equipment. Their faces are streaked with mud and sweat, and their weapons are now fully armed and pointing toward the enemy.

Here we have the same men, but different scenarios. One is ceremonial; the other is combat!

When the legions of Rome came face-to-face with the enemy, the shield was not held close to the body but a little away from it, so that it could be moved up and down to deflect incoming arrows, stones, and other attack ammunition. As soon as the enemy was close enough, then, as a unit, the front line lunged[2] one pace forward, leaning slightly into the enemy. With their weight over the leading leg, so that they could not easily be pushed back, they thrust their shields into the faces or bodies of the enemy, causing the enemy to lose their balance. The shields were then brought back closer to the body, and with a straight jabbing movement, the sword was thrust into the opponent's body. There was no swinging and chopping, just a straight thrust into the vital organs. The front line then moved forward, repeating the process, until the enemy had been vanquished.

Likewise, this is the way to face the devil's attacks. Use the shield of faith to ward off the fiery darts and offensively push it into the face of the devil, so that he is off balance with your heavy use of faith. Then administer the final blow with the sword of the Spirit, not slashing here and there, but deliberately into the body.

> *For the word of God is living and powerful, and sharper than any two-edged sword, **piercing** even to the division of soul and spirit, and of joints and marrow, and is a discerner of the thoughts and intents of the heart* (Hebrews 4:12).

Victory is assured!

> *Resist the devil and he will flee from you* (James 4:7b).

PULLING DOWN STRONGHOLDS

> *For though we walk in the flesh, we do not war according to the flesh. For the weapons of our warfare are not carnal but mighty in God for **pulling down strongholds**, casting down arguments and every high thing that exalts itself against the knowledge of God, bringing every thought into captivity to the obedience of Christ* (2 Corinthians 10:3-5).

Regarding this passage, first realize that we have authority over the forces of darkness only and not over people. No matter who is giving you a hard time, you need to look behind the smoke screen and determine who is the source of the problem, and not through whom it operates.

"Pulling down" is described by the Lord in one of His parables, and it explains clearly the effect that these weapons, which are mighty in God, can achieve.

> *The ground of a certain rich man yielded plentifully. And he thought within himself, saying, "What shall I do, since I have no room to store my crops?" So he said, "I will do this: **I will pull down** my barns and build greater, and there I will store all my crops and my goods"* (Luke 12:16b-18).

This was not knocking a brick or two from the top of the wall. It was a complete leveling of the structure to the ground. This demolition is precisely what is to happen to strongholds and arguments that are opposed to the will of God.

For example, if satan says to you that you are not worthy, you should immediately demolish these thoughts, for they are opposed to the will of God, because Christ has become our righteousness.

> *But of Him you are in Christ Jesus, who became for us wisdom from God—and **righteousness** and sanctification and redemption* (1 Corinthians 1:30).

> *And if Christ is in you, the body is dead because of sin, but the Spirit is life because of **righteousness*** (Romans 8:10).

This argument has to be pulled down, and room made for the truth.

If he says that you are not capable, then again, this argument is demolished by the Word of God:

> *Yet in all these things **we are more than conquerors** through Him who loved us* (Romans 8:37).

This is more than the secular positive confession; this is confessing the Word of God for what it is—God's Word.

Nevertheless, this confession of the Word of God does not mean that we can war for our unsaved loved ones. We cannot claim eternal salvation on their behalf; only they can do that individually. What it does mean though, is that we can come in between, and resist the force that is constantly holding them back. We can pray for them, praying the Word of God into their situation, so that, as the truth of the Gospel is explained to them, God's heart and God's plan comes to fruition in their lives. But for the sake of emphasis, I will repeat again—*you cannot control people by prayer.*

What is a stronghold? A stronghold is nothing more than a castle, a fortress, or a protective wall. It can also be anything on which one relies. A physical stronghold is made with bricks and cement; a spiritual stronghold is built with different materials so that satan is able to contain us. He tries to cause each Christian to become surrounded by a restraining wall that will limit that person's freedom. However, when you are free and Holy Spirit-led, then there are no limitations to you in Christ. Satan is, of course, fully aware of this fact. When you are constrained, and purpose-driven by satan, then you are no threat to his kingdom.

So how does he actually manage to collect all the "bricks" that he needs to build his stronghold?

First of all, the "father of lies" begins by impressing all manner of wrong thoughts into your thought-life—thoughts such as, "They don't love you," or "Someone is saying bad things about you," or any other lies from a multitude of lies. The truth of the matter is, were you to confront those whom you perceive to be the source of the problem and explain how you feel, they would probably be utterly surprised and reveal that there was no truth to base your feeling or thought upon.

I am naturally an encouraging person who loves to inspire and comfort people; however, when I am busy or something is on my mind, I might not hear or be aware of what is going on around me. In the past, some of my coworkers have thought that I was upset about something they had done. Yet it could not have been further from the truth. I told them clearly, "If you have done something wrong, I will tell you. And if I have said nothing, then you can take it that nothing is wrong. I just happened to have something completely different on my mind."

Secondly, satan starts to isolate individual Christians. Once they are alone, they become more vulnerable. Their minds can be influenced quite easily, and without the benefit of good teaching and the support of other believers, they fall prey to his allurements.

For example, a person might begin to think that there is a whispering campaign about him or her. Then, one Sunday morning, the pastor greets some people but neglects to acknowledge that person. Right away, satan attacks their mind with, *Does the pastor have something against me? And why is that sister looking at me like that? What is she thinking?*

Gradually, the gall of bitterness creeps in, and the bricks begin to mount up with which satan can build his stronghold around that person. Often I find that people pray, "Oh Lord, please speak to my leader concerning this or that." Prayer is good; it is blessed. But leaders are not mind readers. You could save yourself a lot of trouble if you would just do what the Word says:

Therefore if you bring your gift to the altar, and there remember that your brother has something against you, leave your gift there before the altar, and go your way. First be reconciled to your brother, and then come and offer your gift (Matthew 5:23-24).

The same applies if you have something against somebody or think that they have something against you. Go and talk to the person, and you might be surprised to find that there is no substance to those feelings at all.

Pursue peace with all people, and holiness, without which no one will see the Lord: looking carefully lest anyone fall short of the grace of God; **lest any root of bitterness springing up cause trouble,** *and by this many become defiled* (Hebrews 12:14-15).

Satan has his bricks, and the cement to bind them together comes from within the person who allows these thoughts to grow and multiply. Agreement has power in the positive or the negative. Whatever you agree with in both cases shall be done to you. The brick represents the thought, while meditating on the thought and agreeing with it is the cement that binds it together.

A good man out of the good treasure of his heart brings forth good; and an evil man out of the evil treasure of his heart brings forth evil. For out of the abundance of the heart his mouth speaks (Luke 6:45).

But those things which proceed out of the mouth come from the heart, and they defile a man (Matthew 15:18).

And the **tongue** *is a fire, a world of iniquity. The* **tongue** *is so set among our members that it defiles the whole body, and sets on fire the course of nature; and it is set on fire by hell* (James 3:6).

Every attack of the devil now bears hard upon this person, as the bricks and mortar are built up around the individual. Now, the child of God has a choice. Apply the Word, confess the Scriptures, resist the enemy, and find freedom. Or if he chooses not to react this way, then the thoughts become a part of his feelings, actions, and language, which will take his focus away from God and put it squarely on the problem. The result is a very unstable Christian walk.

This Christian might still be encased in his heavenly armor, but there is a wall surrounding both him and his armor. He might be able to move his shield and lunge with his sword, but it is only within the stronghold that satan has erected around him! He can move around within the confines of the fortress but cannot move outside of it. He is limited in his effectiveness to advance the Kingdom of God, and his witness to the effectiveness of the Gospel is hampered. He is restrained and not free in Christ Jesus (see Rom. 8:2).

You can prophesy, you can worship, you can preach, you can still do many things; but you cannot advance, because there is a stronghold in some part of your mind, put there by yourself in allowing the thoughts of satan to reside there.

You might be a mighty, powerful preacher.

You might be an evangelist.

You might be a man or woman of God.

You might be operating in a certain gifting.

Nevertheless, satan has blocked you in!

This is the stronghold that has to be pulled down, that has to be demolished. The equipment assigned to us by Almighty God are the shield of faith and the sword of the Spirit—and both have to be used aggressively, not against fellow believers, but against the powers of darkness. We are no longer under satan's orders; we are in the Kingdom of the Son of God.

> *He has delivered us from the power of darkness and conveyed us into the kingdom of the Son of His love* (Colossians 1:13).

The Word of God *must be applied*, not just read and agreed, but put into practice. If the Word of God says that you are a child of God (and it does), then live your life victoriously as a child of God.

> *But as many as received Him, to them He gave the right to become **children of God**, to those who believe in His name* (John 1:12).

> *The Spirit Himself bears witness with our spirit that **we are children of God*** (Romans 8:16).

Demolishing a building involves more than just a tacit agreement that there is no structure left standing! It takes effort, willpower, and time, but once these have been employed, the building is soon leveled.

As it is in the natural, so it is in the spiritual. You have all the equipment required for pulling down the strongholds that the enemy has built up around you, but they have to be used, and only you can use them. Set to, and watch the results!

CAST DOWN ARGUMENTS AND BRING EVERY THOUGHT INTO CAPTIVITY

Let's consider the following Scripture passage from three different versions:

> For though we walk in the flesh, we do not war according to the flesh. For the weapons of our warfare are not carnal but mighty in God for pulling down strongholds, **casting down arguments and every high thing that exalts itself against the knowledge of God, bringing every thought into captivity to the obedience of Christ**, and being ready to punish all disobedience when your obedience is fulfilled (2 Corinthians 10:3-6).

> We are human, but we don't wage war with human plans and methods. We use God's mighty weapons, not mere worldly weapons, to knock down the devil's strongholds. With these weapons we **break down every proud argument that keeps people from knowing God. With these weapons we conquer their rebellious ideas, and we teach them to obey Christ**. And after you have become fully obedient, we will punish everyone who remains disobedient (2 Corinthians 10:3-6 NLT).

> For though we walk (live) in the flesh, we are not carrying on our warfare according to the flesh and using mere human weapons. For the weapons of our warfare are not physical [weapons of flesh and blood], but they are mighty before God for the overthrow and destruction of strongholds, [inasmuch as we] **refute arguments and theories and reasonings and every proud and lofty thing that sets itself up against the [true] knowledge of God; and we lead every thought and purpose away captive into the obedience of Christ** (the Messiah, the Anointed One), being in readiness to punish every [insubordinate for his] disobedience, when your own submission and obedience [as a church] are fully secured and complete (2 Corinthians 10:3-6 AMP).

We have seen in the former passage that strongholds are walls. How are these strongholds built? Through the thoughts that we allow in our mind. The Amplified Bible calls them "theories and reasonings."

When a thought comes into the mind, is it from God or from the enemy? If it is ultimately to the glory of God or the building of God's Kingdom, then it is from Him. However, if it ultimately honors man, or moves the perspective from God to self, then it is from the enemy. All thoughts that oppose the Word of God are from satan.

Ask yourself, "Did this thought just come into my mind, or was it from deep in my spirit?" Thoughts from the enemy will be loud and hasty, whereas thoughts from the Spirit of God will be as a still small voice that repeatedly nudges you.

These false arguments of the enemy are dealt with in the same manner as the strongholds. They are repulsed and knocked off balance by the shield of faith, and then they are destroyed by the sword of the Spirit. In simple words, pray the Word of God irrespective of your feelings at all times.

Often, ungodly thoughts will persist, no matter how many times the Christian tries to get rid of them. The secret is, keep resisting, try to fill your mind with worship, and praying in tongues (if you do). That way, we take authority over that thought, and in reality make it a prisoner, as we take it to the Word of God. It is important that we fill our minds and lives with spiritual topics, worship, and reading of the Word. It should not be worldly, fleshly programs and scenes that fill our thoughts; otherwise, these ungodly thoughts will have a fertile breeding ground in which to grow and develop.

Personally, I have a very vivid imagination, and most of the time, I remember in pictures. I quickly learned that I could not easily get rid of the pictures of some movie or program that I had I watched on TV. It was not necessarily evil; but even so, it filled my thought life and it took some discipline to get rid of its powerful grip on my mind. I realized that the choice was mine; what I allow my eyes to see, my mind will produce. Sexual sin always starts first in the thought life before it manifests in the natural. These thoughts require a firm covenant not to watch those things and to switch off the TV when they occur, and that you take authority over those thoughts, no matter what scheme satan is hatching.

Let the word of Christ dwell in you richly in all wisdom, teaching and admonishing one another in psalms and hymns and spiritual songs, singing with grace in your hearts to the Lord (Colossians 3:16).

When the Christian obeys the injunctions of the Word of God, perverse thoughts have a difficult time in establishing themselves. They will still come; the fiery darts are a constant bombardment, but like the seed that fell on barren ground, they will not bear fruit.

I learned these things through the hardships and mistakes of my own life. Some 30 years ago, as a young, born-again, Spirit-filled missionary working for God, I could quote the Word and knew many portions of it by rote. I was a new creation and a conqueror. At least, that is what the Bible told me, although at that time, I only lived it in part. In theory, it was correct, but in practice, I failed hopelessly. My spiritual life was an emotional roller coaster. One wrong word and I could be in the depth of disappointment, or one encouraging word, and I was on top of the world. Nobody would have dreamed that I was in the grips of the deepest inferiority complex that you could imagine. I looked as if I had everything together, but deep within I was an emotional wreck.

Nobody could ever know how many nights I spent on my knees before God seeking His help, and all because, as a child I grew up as the ugly duckling of the family. Several negative things had been spoken about me that seriously affected my life. Now of course, my family had never meant to hurt me. I do not think that they even realized what effect their words had on me, even to the very core of my being. No matter how hard I tried, whatever I did was simply not good enough.

Later on, by training, I became a registered nurse and a midwife, but even in my employment, I worked night and day to prove myself to those around me. I became a workaholic and a hard-driven perfectionist. Then, I became a Christian. I read that I was a "new creation," but what did that really mean? I did not understand, and there was nobody who could explain to me "the liberty that we have in Christ Jesus."

So what happened? Remember that I was and still am in full-time Christian work. As I stood on the platform, I looked confident, sounded confident, and exuded a certain professionalism. Yet nobody discerned that I had serious problems. I cried out to God repeatedly, "Lord, help me! Set me free!" I wonder how many times Jesus looked down from His throne at this pitiful person and said, "You have the sword in your hand; just take it and use it. I have given you the authority." How many times must He have said, "Come on, Suzette, you have the armor. I have paid all your debts. Rise up with the sword; rise up with the Word of God; and start fighting back. Resist the devil!" Nevertheless, I did not know what to do. I did not know how to resist. I did not know how to fight back, and so I went from bad to worse.

I went through periods of high spirits, followed by times of feeling so low that I did not think that I would ever get up. My entire spiritual life was like a yo-yo, up and down all the time.

In the meantime, in the mission organization where I worked, there was a lady, a dear child of God, who, because of an abnormality of her spine, was physically built small. When you compared the size of the two of us, we were like David and Goliath—I towered over her. What aggravated me more than anything with this lady was the fact that I thought that she did not like me! It seemed to me that she was always attacking me with her tongue. Finally, I said to God, "God, I cannot live like this anymore—this inferiority; and my emotions being constantly like a roller coaster are destroying me."

So, I went up into the mountains to a small house. I locked the door, I fasted, and I prayed. It was God, me, fresh water, fresh air, and my Bible. I began to cry out to the Lord to set me free from this bondage.

Days passed. Weeks passed. And then one day, I came upon this Scripture—Second Corinthians 10:3-6. It took me completely by surprise. I had read it so many times, but this time the Spirit of God illuminated it to my understanding. I had never heard teaching on it. Strongholds! What were strongholds? Take every thought captive! Slowly I began to understand— *it was not what people were doing to me. It was the thoughts in my own mind that were causing my emotional roller coaster.*

These were the arguments, theories, and reasonings that Second Corinthians 10:5 was talking about. Let us stop looking for demons behind every person and rock. Let us deal with the strongholds in our own minds; then, the Body of Christ and satan will not know where to hide from this victorious army!

Gradually, I began to understand just what satan was doing in my life and in the lives of my brothers and sisters in Christ. He was constantly pointing me back to what I used to be, what my achievements were in my own strength, how I perceived my preaching to be. In other words, he turned my focus from Jesus onto myself.

The psalmist put my understanding into true perspective when he wrote,

> *The entrance of Your words gives light; it gives understanding to the simple* (Psalm 119:130).

I was angry, I was annoyed; in fact, I was livid with the devil for having manipulated me for so long. I said, "Satan, you will never do this to me again! Never!"

That morning changed my life forever. I became a woman of the Word—not just preaching it, reading it, and quoting it, but living it with every inch of my physical and spiritual life. Obviously, as a missionary, I had preached the Word before, but that morning, the Word of God became a tool—it became my sword. The more I practiced wielding it, the more proficient I became.

I began to say what the Word of God has to say about me. I began to confess it over my life; I began to pray it; I used it constantly. I changed my mind to come in line with what the Word of God says about me, and not what I said about myself!

I came back from that mountain retreat excited and ready to do battle for the Lord, but I first had to pass an unexpected test. Who should be the first person to meet me on my return but the tiny lady! I said, "Lord, is this really necessary?" She came to me, and immediately the old feelings of inferiority, rejection, and not being good enough, began to rise up inside of me. At that same moment, my spirit arose within me, and I thought to myself, *Oh no, satan, you will not do this to me again!* Being a young Christian, I did not really know how to react, and all I could think of that moment was to hug her as tight as I could. She was small and I was tall, so this was quite a sight to see. I said, "Susan, let me tell you what Jesus has done for me!"

We sat down together and I began to tell her everything that had taken place up in the mountains. Soon, she too was crying, because she also was hiding behind her walls on account of her size. We started praying together, and pulled down those strongholds. We became the best of friends and at one time, we both shared an apartment together.

We might have looked like David and Goliath, but we became more like David and Jonathan.

Did the devil ever attack me after that? Of course he did; he had that territory for a long time, but now I am learning to stand my ground and possess that which Christ has won for me on Calvary. At first, it was difficult. However, I began to understand that I must reinforce each victory over the devil. The weapons that we are given must be used in a sensible manner. You do not find professional soldiers waving their rifles all over the place and firing indiscriminately. Not only is that a waste of ammunition but it can also kill friendly forces. No, those weapons are pointed toward the enemy, and every round of ammunition is made to count.

Again, as it is in the natural, so it is in the spiritual. Use the shield of faith as a defensive weapon and also as an offensive weapon. The sword of the Spirit, the Word of God, is to be used forcefully, in a direct lunge against the enemy.

Currently, I have seen hundreds and thousands of people being set free by the understanding of this simple teaching, which I have put it into five points. It is not a recipe, just a guideline; do not worry if you do not get it right. Simply pray out of your spirit and take authority.

1. Start with worship.

2. Resist the enemy.

3. Take authority over every thought.

4. Cast each one down and pull down the stronghold.

5. Pray the Word of God. For example:

    Father, I worship You. I submit myself to You, and declare and confess that Jesus is my Lord and Savior. Satan, you spirit of fear and inferiority, in the name of Jesus, I take authority over your lies in my mind, and also in the name of Jesus. I cast down these thoughts, and break every stronghold around me. I am climbing out of my stronghold, and I demolish these vain imaginations concerning me. I am more than a conqueror; in Christ Jesus I can do all things. Whom the Son has set free is free indeed.

Now continue to worship the Lord. Do not expect to feel anything. You should not be governed by feelings but by faith. Continue to pray until it becomes an absolute part or revelation to your spirit.

ENDNOTES

1. Words and music: Helen H. Lemmel, 1922.

2. In fencing—an attack made by extending the rear leg and landing on the bent front leg.

CHAPTER 5

Prayers That Bring Forth Fruit

THIS CHAPTER IS WRITTEN OUT of a deep longing in my heart to have greater results and an abundance of fruit in my prayer life. For many years, I had led intercession, and yet I came to a place where I cried out to God all the more for greater impact, more clarity, and increased fruitfulness.

Like the disciples, I pleaded, "Lord, teach me to pray!" I did not need a new anointing; I simply wanted to put that indwelling anointing to better use, to more fruitful use, to more effective use.

Then the Lord, through the Holy Spirit, began to do just what I had asked. A passage of Scripture would begin to flow through my spirit night after night, day after day, and the Holy Spirit would then open my understanding so that I could grasp what He wanted to communicate to me.

BLESSED OR FRUITFUL?

There is a significant difference between a blessed life and a fruitful life. The Bible tells us that we are blessed.

> *Blessed be the God and Father of our Lord Jesus Christ, **who has blessed us with every spiritual blessing** in the heavenly places in Christ* (Ephesians 1:3).

Therefore, if you are a child of God serving Jesus Christ, you are blessed. However, being blessed does not mean that you are fruitful. Being fruitful is something completely different.

Let us look at the first Psalm:

> Blessed is the man who walks not in the counsel of the ungodly, nor stands in the path of sinners, nor sits in the seat of the scornful; but his delight is in the law of the Lord, and in His law he meditates day and night. He shall be like a tree planted by the rivers of water, that brings forth its fruit in its season, whose leaf also shall not wither; and whatever he does shall prosper (Psalm 1:1-3).

The first verse portrays the normal Christian life. "Blessed is the man who walks not in the counsel of the ungodly, nor stands in the path of sinners, nor sits in the seat of the scornful." This verse represents (or should represent) our everyday life as a Christian. We are human, and we live in a human world. Nevertheless, that does not mean that we are of the world.

> Now we have received, not the spirit of the world, but the Spirit who is from God, that we might know the things that have been freely given to us by God (1 Corinthians 2:12).

The psalmist here draws a clear distinction between being blessed (verse 1) and being fruitful to the point that whatever you do or lay your hands on will prosper (verses 2-3). And as always, the promise of God comes with a condition.

> His delight is in the law of the Lord, and in His law he meditates day and night. He shall be like a tree planted by the rivers of water, that brings forth its fruit in its season, whose leaf also shall not wither; and whatever he does shall prosper (Psalm 1:2-3).

Here we see the Christians' delight, which if indulged in, results in fruitfulness—as trees planted by the river. The trees that grow by the side of a river are often willows. Their wood is used for furniture making, and the withes (the long tough stems) are used in wickerwork. Willows are very flexible and can be twisted and bent as desired. This is a picture of the Christian, who is flexible under the guidance of the Holy Spirit and can be easily moved to fulfill His purposes.

The Bible tells us that these trees will yield their fruit in season. What does "brings forth its fruit in its season" mean? It means that you will bring forth the fruit desired from you at that specific moment in the situation. In other words, when God wants you to cry out, you cry out. When God wants you for a prophetic purpose, you utter the words that He gives. When a testimony is needed, you give it. Bringing forth fruit in season means that God can use you for His purpose whenever He desires in whatever situation. It might mean a mere hug, a simple word of encouragement, a prayer, or a word spoken in due season. But the Scripture goes on to say, "Whatever he does shall prosper"! In other words, it shall succeed; it will work!

MEDITATING OUT LOUD

The key words to ensure fruitfulness and spiritual prosperity are given in verse 2. This is of utter importance to note and understand!

*His **delight** is in the law of the Lord, and in His law he **meditates** day and night* (Psalm 1:2).

The word "meditation" has several definitions; let us see what the Bible means here.

The word "meditate" in Hebrew is *hagah*, which is pronounced "haw-gaw," and it has a very interesting meaning—"to reflect, to mourn, to mutter, to ponder, to meditate, or contemplate something as one repeats the words." *Hagah* represents something quite unlike the English "meditation," which is mainly a mental exercise, understood as:

- Thinking deeply.
- Continuous or successful concentration.
- Uninterrupted thoughts on a subject.

In the Hebrew, it relates to a practical, active, audible process, one in which the mind, the will, the emotions, and the voice are all employed. The Hebrew concept of "meditation" is to take a portion of Scripture and quietly vocalize it, while completely abandoning outside distractions. In this type of meditation, the Word of God is prayed back to Him aloud.

In order to prove from Scripture that *hagah* is a vocal response, the following examples are used as proof texts. There are many verses, but this is purposely done so that you can reassess your understanding of what it is to meditate. Read every verse and ponder the italicized portions, which are a translation of *hagah*.

> *This Book of the Law shall not depart from your mouth, but you* **shall meditate** *in it day and night, that you may observe to do according to all that is written in it. For then you will make your way prosperous, and then you will have good success* (Joshua 1:8).

> *But his delight is in the law of the Lord, and in His law he* **meditates** *day and night* (Psalm 1:2).

> *And my tongue* **shall speak** *of Your righteousness and of Your praise all the day long* (Psalm 35:28).

> *When I remember You on my bed, I* **meditate** *on You in the night watches* (Psalm 63:6).

> *I* **will** *also* **meditate** *on all Your work, and talk of Your deeds* (Psalm 77:12).

> *I remember the days of old; I* **meditate** *on all Your works; I muse on the work of Your hands* (Psalm 143:5).

> *Like a crane or a swallow, so I chattered; I* **mourned** *like a dove; my eyes fail from looking upward. O Lord, I am oppressed; undertake for me!* (Isaiah 38:14)

> *For your hands are defiled with blood, and your fingers with iniquity; your lips have spoken lies, your tongue* **has muttered** *perversity* (Isaiah 59:3).

> *Therefore I will wail for Moab, and I will cry out for all Moab; I* **will mourn** *for the men of Kir Heres* (Jeremiah 48:31).

Plotting, planning, roaring, speaking, mourning, muttering—these are all vocal actions. Thus, it is with the voice that one meditates; it is not just a mental exercise.

PRAYING THE WORD OF GOD

So, who will bring forth fruit? Those who pray out loud the Word of God back to Him during their prayer time! The Scriptures here are not merely suggesting quoting a Scripture now and then to the Lord or proclaiming some Scripture into the situation.

The Hebrew here suggests that you take the very Word of God, verse by verse, and pray that aloud, not just as a quotation, but as the essence of your prayer back to God—not just reminding Him of His promises for some situation, but to make the Word of God your very prayer. This does not mean that you should not ever generally converse with God, but it does mean that a great portion of your prayer is *pure Scripture!*

"But there is nothing new in this practice," you might say. "I regularly pray the Scriptures." Or do you? Perhaps you have been quoting Scripture back to Almighty God, a promise here, a promise there, or a favorite verse. Think about it! You might pray in the spirit, in tongues, or you might pray with your understanding; you might spend time in praise and worship. And all those prayers are wonderful. But if you want to be fruitful or be like a tree planted next to the waters, then, according to Psalm 1:2, you must meditate (vocalize), pray out loud the Scriptures back to God.

Allow me to give you an example of how I pray the Word back to the Lord. Please understand that I am *not* saying that the Spirit does not lead the way you have been praying. I'm simply relaying that I have found this way to be extremely effective and to have great impact. As you progress in your prayer life, the Holy Spirit will lead you to your own individual style of praying the Word of God.

> *The Spirit of the Lord God is upon Me, because the Lord has anointed Me to preach good tidings to the poor; He has sent Me to heal the brokenhearted, to proclaim liberty to the captives, and the opening of the prison to those who are bound* (Isaiah 61:1).

Following is an example of how I would pray the verse, Isaiah 61:1:

> *Father, I thank You this day that Your Holy Spirit indwells me, and even though I might not feel as strong today, Lord, Your Spirit still empowers me. Thank You that You are always at Your highest point of strength, even within me, Lord, for there is no shadow of turning with You. Thank You that Your anointing not only indwells me, but that You have anointed me to preach good news to the poor. You have sent me, Lord, and I accept that calling to heal the brokenhearted and to proclaim the freedom to the captives! In Jesus' name, I open those prison doors of drug addiction, of alcohol, of confusion, of sickness; I speak to them in*

Jesus' name. I submit myself to God and resist the enemy, and command those prison doors to open….

Now imagine going on to verse 2 and then 3…before you know it, time has flown by. Sometimes when I lead group prayer, I will also pray Scripture but break it up. For example:

Arise, shine; for your light has come! And the glory of the Lord is risen upon you (Isaiah 60:1).

Arise.

Arise in taking authority in your prayer life.

Arise in more worship.

Arise in commitment in daily devotions.

Shine.

Shine in your testimony for Jesus Christ.

Shine in being active in practical evangelism.

Glory.

Signs and wonders in the Church.

Healing for the sick.

Anointing in the meetings.

These are very simple examples. You likewise can take any promise that God has given you, and divide it into parts for you or the group to pray. This makes praying the Word exciting and manageable for the strongest or weakest prayer warrior. This is *hagah* in a different form.

Some Practical Advice

If there is a specific verse that touches my heart or draws my attention as I am daily reading the Bible, I will start praying that one verse back to God. "Lord, talk to me about this. What do You want me to understand in this verse?" Then I will read the verse or passage out loud to Him. We now have communication, not just a monologue. "Father, this word really touches my heart—'Blessed is the man.' Thank You, Father, that You are blessing us in Your love, and that in Deuteronomy 28, You have said, 'Blessed is your coming in and your going out; blessed are you in the basket; blessed are you in the field.' "

I might feel strongly that the Holy Spirit wants me to pray only one word in that verse or perhaps the entire passage. Hence, my prayer has direction, and is specific. It is an excellent way to increase your prayer life when you do not know what to continue to say. Often, we long to spend more time in prayer, but we do not know how. Start by praying the Psalms, or your devotion passage of the day. Soon, you will find hours passing by. This is also an excellent way to motivate your own spirit when you do not feel like praying! Praying the Word out loud motivates faith, for faith comes by hearing and hearing the Word of the Lord!

The tradition of this style of prayer has been practiced over centuries by the Jewish people and is a specialized type of prayer known as "davening" prayer, which is reciting text, praying intense prayers, getting lost in communion with God while bowing or rocking back and forth. Evidently, this dynamic form of meditation goes back to David's time.

No Empty Hands

In the light of the power of *hagah* (praying God's Word back), Isaiah 55:11 has a complete new meaning. Here we see that *it is impossible for God's Word to return without results*!

> *So shall My word be that goes forth from My mouth;* **it shall not return to Me void**, *but it shall accomplish what I please, and it shall prosper in the thing for which I sent it* (Isaiah 55:11).

Please note, in order to ascertain the correct meaning of the word "void" in this Scripture, we must look at the Hebrew meaning. Today's definition of the word is unlike that of the Old Testament Hebrew. A modern definition of "void" is the state of nonexistence, or an empty area or space. Yet none of these definitions fit the concept as presented by Isaiah. In most Bibles, at Isaiah 55:11, the words "without fruit" are inserted next to the word "void." So, what is the Word saying?

> *So shall My word be that goes forth from My mouth;* **it shall not return to Me void** [without fruit], *but it shall accomplish what I please, and it shall prosper in the thing for which I sent it* (Isaiah 55:11).

This sheds complete new light on the praying of the Word. It shall not return void or without fruit, but it shall come back with fruit.

In determining the significance of the word "meditate," several verses of Scripture were adduced in order to provide the correct meaning. The same applies in the case of "void." Please read all the following verses carefully, because it is in the understanding of this word "void" (not an empty wilderness, but fruitless) that the power of meditation (that is, praying the Word of God with an anticipated fruitful harvest) becomes apparent.

The emphasized words in bold are the same Hebrew word.

> And I will give this people favor in the sight of the Egyptians; and it shall be, when you go, that you shall not go **empty-handed** (Exodus 3:21).

> And when you send him away free from you, you shall not let him go away **empty-handed** (Deuteronomy 15:13).

> I went out full, and the Lord has brought me home again **empty**. Why do you call me Naomi, since the Lord has testified against me, and the Almighty has afflicted me? (Ruth 1:21)

> And she said, "These six ephahs of barley he gave me; for he said to me, 'Do not go **empty-handed** to your mother-in-law'" (Ruth 3:17).

In those verses, the word "void" occurs only once! The recurring theme is that of being empty-handed. It is nothing to do with empty existence, but everything to do with lack of fruit. To return from a shopping spree empty-handed means that you did not buy anything; there was no "fruit" from your shopping.

As we now reflect upon what Isaiah said about the Word of God, we can change this to read:

> So shall My word be that goes forth from My mouth; **it shall not return to Me empty-handed** [without fruit], but it shall accomplish what I please, and it shall prosper in the thing for which I sent it (Isaiah 55:11).

In other words, as the Word of God returns to Him, it bears the fruit for which He has sent it to prosper. That is the power of praying God's Word.

How many times do we pray for this or that, pray for revival or pray for healing, and nothing seems to happen? We begin to wonder to ourselves, *When is God going to answer?* Let me ask you a question: How much Scripture have you been praying into that situation? Every prayer is a seed planted in the harvest field of God. Thus,

EVERY PRAYER IS A SEED PLANTED IN THE HARVEST FIELD OF GOD.

if we want to see miracles, then we need to plant miracle seeds. If someone needs healing, then we must plant healing seeds; if there is a need for salvation, then planting salvation seeds is what is required. All these seeds are contained in the Word of God, which are prayed back to Him, not by repetition, not by formula, but by earnest, Holy Spirit guided prayer.

LOGOS

There are two terms used in the New Testament to designate the term "word"—*logos* and *rhema*. *Logos* is the general Word of God. The following example shows a *logos* type of prayer.

Once, I was talking to the Lord about something that was on my heart. I could have continued reading my Bible, but I felt that I needed something more than just reading. So I sat there, hugging my Bible, and I said, "Lord, I do not quite understand this, but I really need an answer from You concerning a dear friend who has been in an accident." There was no specific Scripture coming to my mind, but, because I had studied the Word of God, I knew of several Scriptures on healing by heart. I started quoting them, praying them out loud, I *hagah*-ed before God, knowing that it is impossible for the Word of God not to have effect, as Isaiah 55:11 promises us. I simply took my general knowledge of healing Scriptures and started praying them. Soon, the Holy Spirit enlightened a Scripture to me that actually had nothing to do with healing but was the perfect Scripture for the situation—which leads me to the *rhema*.

RHEMA

Rhema is the "quickened," the "enlightened," the "now" Word of God. It is a portion of the *logos* that has been revealed and made alive to us by the Holy Spirit as an answer to or for a specific situation.

The best way to illustrate a *rhema* word is by means of the following picture along with an explanation.

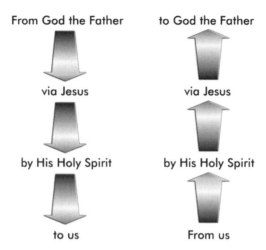

*For **through Him** [Jesus] we both have access **by one Spirit to the Father*** (Ephesians 2:18).

This verse gives us the dynamic of our relationship with the Godhead—*through* Jesus, by the Holy Spirit, to our heavenly Father. And the reverse is also true—*from* the Father, *through* Jesus, His Son, then *by* the Holy Spirit *to* us! This is why Jesus died on the cross, so that those who believe in Him can have communion with the Father.

> *That which we have seen and heard we declare to you, that you also may have fellowship with us; and truly **our fellowship is with the Father and with His Son Jesus Christ*** (1 John 1:3).

Jesus is seated at the right hand of the Father, interceding for the saints.

> *Who is he who condemns? It is Christ who died, and furthermore is also risen, who is even **at the right hand of God**, who also **makes intercession** for us* (Romans 8:34).

The Holy Spirit is not only our comforter, our helper, and advocate, but also an intercessor.

> *Likewise the Spirit also helps in our weaknesses. For we do not know what we should pray for as we ought, but **the Spirit Himself makes intercession for us** with groanings which cannot be uttered. Now He who searches the hearts knows what the mind of the Spirit is, because He makes intercession for the saints according to the will of God* (Romans 8:26-27).

Child of God, you have nothing to fear. Two of the most powerful intercessors of all times are praying for you by name—Jesus and the Holy Spirit! They are always in line with the Father's will, and their prayers are always answered! For you and me to be more effective in our intercession, the secret is to find out what Jesus and the Holy Spirit are praying (see Rom. 8:34,26), and to join in with them. Coming in line with their prayers assures results.

How can we know what Jesus and the Holy Spirit are praying? It is quite simple—I call it "the law of agreement," which is clearly shown in the following Scripture:

> However, when He, the Spirit of truth, has come, He will guide you into all truth; for **He will not speak on His own authority, but whatever He hears He will speak; and He will tell you things to come.** He will glorify Me, for He will take of what is Mine and declare it to you. All things that the Father has are Mine. Therefore I said that He will take of Mine and declare it to you (John 16:13-15).

In this passage, we see the interaction of the whole Godhead. Jesus is interceding for us at the right hand of the Father. The Holy Spirit listens to the dialogue and then reveals to us that which He has heard. The things that the Holy Spirit speaks concern those matters that have passed between Jesus and the Father and vice versa. He does not speak on His own authority but tells us what He has heard spoken in the throne room of God concerning you and me! God shares His secrets (Psalm 25:14). He loves to drop hints concerning His great plans for you; He does so through the Holy Spirit telling you "things to come," which is prophetic, the future, the revealed Word of God for your situation—the *rhema*.

In order to explain in practical detail how this comes about, I want you to imagine the following scenario.

As I am interceding concerning a specific matter, I say, "Father, in the name of Jesus, show me by Your Holy Spirit what is on Your heart." Jesus then intercedes with the Father, and the Holy Spirit listens to what is taking place. The Father responds to His Son's prayers and answers Him. The Holy Spirit takes what He has just heard, and as I am reading my Bible, He points out a significant passage or verse, which seems to "leap up off the page," or it becomes a revelation to me.

This revelation might come as a song, a reminder of a verse of Scripture, or it might even come through another person with a specific passage of Scripture on their heart just for me. All of these are means and ways that the Holy Spirit uses.

That passage or verse is now the *rhema* Word. It is the revealed, enlightened, and specific passage for a specific situation. This is exciting. It is dealing with your future prophetically, and above all, you are led into the secrets of God that concern you.

Now that we have this *rhema* Word, what are we to do with it? We all have these special promises; they are underlined in our Bibles with a date, or they are collated in a journal. We have Scripture after Scripture, which are highlighted and noted with thanks, yet remain fixed on the page and not activated into fruit-producing prayer. Remember the verse from Isaiah 55 that we quoted earlier? This now comes into play.

> *So shall My word be that goes forth from My mouth;* **it shall not return to Me void** *[empty-handed, without fruit], but it shall accomplish what I please, and it shall prosper in the thing for which I sent it* (Isaiah 55:11).

The Word of God is "returned" to Him by praying it. As soon as you start to pray the *rhema* Word in meditation (*hagah*)—by praying aloud, then Heaven comes in action. The Holy Spirit takes the Scripture as you vocalize it, and because He is a creative Spirit, He uses those words to create the fruit for which you are praying. That is the power of prayer!

> *Man lives by* **every word that proceeds from the mouth of the Lord** (Deuteronomy 8:3c).

> *And* **I have put My words in your mouth**; *I have covered you with the shadow of My hand,* **that I may plant the heavens, lay the foundations of the earth, and say to Zion,** *"You are My people"* (Isaiah 51:16).

> *But He answered and said, "It is written, 'Man shall not live by bread alone, but by* **every word that proceeds from the mouth of God'"** (Matthew 4:4).

THE POWER OF AGREEMENT

For the sake of clarity, I want to summarize this most important teaching.

The burden comes from the Father; Jesus intercedes for that burden at the right hand of the Father; and the Holy Spirit, who listens to that conversation, then brings it to us and begins to burden our hearts, or encourages us with a *rhema* Word. Now we are involved, and we start closing the circle by *hagah*. We pray that Scripture back to God, and because it is impossible for it not to bear fruit or have an impact, the Holy Spirit now carries that prayer back to the Father in the name of Jesus!

The circle is fulfilled because it has originated and ended with Father God. He answers the prayer—the power of agreement.

How do you know whether you are praying the correct Scripture verse, so that it can return to the Father bearing fruit? The Holy Spirit indwells you, and He will remind you of the Scriptures that you have stored in your spirit through reading and studying God's Word. He is a faithful Spirit, who searches the deep things of God, and so He will give you a peace and joy in your spirit, an excitement, or a deep inner knowledge that you are following His will.

I would like to make it very clear that you do not have to wait until you have a rhema Word in order to pray the Scriptures. Whatever your need, pray the promises of God over it, irrespective of whether those scriptural promises have been enlightened to you or not. The Holy Spirit will take those Scriptures and reveal them to you in due course, or He may give you a totally different passage as a rhema for your need.

> *If you abide in Me, and My words* [rhema] *abide in you, you will ask what you desire, and it shall be done for you. By this My Father is glorified, that you bear much fruit; so you will be My disciples* (John 15:7-8).

The more the rhema words are prayed, the more effective is the law of agreement and the greater the harvest.

Suppose you have been praying, and praying all the rhema words that you have been given, and yet nothing happens? Will it really work? Yes! Our task is to pray and believe until the last second.

Nevertheless, when the Son of Man comes, **will He really find faith on the earth**? (Luke 18:8b)

I always say, "Faith is believing that God is in charge even when it does not look like it."

When you are going through a difficult time, I personally advise you to read the Psalms! Read as much as you can; keep reading until you find your feelings or emotions reflected in a Psalm. Now, carefully read that Psalm again, because somewhere in those verses is the solution to your situation. Read the Psalm aloud before God (*hagah*), as if it were your very own cry from the heart. Then read, and claim for yourself the promise that God gave to the psalmist for his situation. This is also *your* promise for *your* situation. Reading the Psalms this way has helped me in countless situations.

People often come to me and say, "I have prayed the Scriptures for my sick loved one and I have claimed the prophecies. Why then did God not heal this person?" I truly do not have an answer for you, except that I know that it is both my and your responsibility and privilege to hold on in faith until the last second. My job is to believe; His job is to do the miracle according to His prerogative. Once again, when we stand before Him, "will He really find faith on the earth?"

Yes, He will, for we will keep on believing in active faith!

Let us now combine all that we have learned in this chapter, and apply it through prayer. As an example, let's start with John 15:7-8.

> *If you abide in Me* [walk, stand, and sit with Him—Psalm 1], *and My words* [rhema—specific, or enlightened words] *abide in you* [if you pray them and meditate on them, *hagah* them out loud], *you will ask* [according to those rhema words] *what you desire, and it shall be done for you* (John 15:7).
>
> *Then you will be like a tree planted next to the waters, you will be flexible in the guidance of God and whatever you lay your hands on will prosper in the Lord* (Psalm 1:3; author's paraphrase).
>
> *By this My Father is glorified, that you bear much fruit; so you will be My disciples* (John 15:8).

MORE POWER FOR YOUR CHURCH

If you are a pastor or a leader of a group of Christians, find out what promises or prophecies have been given to your church or group. If these have been tested and found to be of God (not just good ideas), then write them down and distribute them to your congregation or group—one at a time for a specific period.

Once a week, during your main service, take time to pray these Scripture verses into being, either corporately or in groups of twos or threes. Put them on the overhead, print them out on papers, and encourage the entire church to come in agreement with the intercession of Jesus and the Holy Spirit. This will bring your whole church or group into unity with the plans of the Godhead for your church, group, or situation.

How exciting our prayer meetings would be if we prayed a lot more Scripture! If we prayed all the prophetic words given to us by God, it would bring faith, excitement, and involvement. This is, of course, also true individually. I often travel, and therefore, I do not always have somebody to pray with me. However, I know that the Holy Spirit is a person, the Word of God is a person; thus, we pray together promise after promise over my team, my life, our finances, and our calling. And it has had tremendous impact. Do that and await a prosperous harvest.

CHAPTER 6

Travail

Then being with child, she cried out in labor and in pain to give birth (Revelation 12:2).

ONE OF THE PARTS OF intercession is travail, which the dictionary defines as: "the concluding state of pregnancy, from the onset of labor to the birth of a child—the use of physical or mental energy—hard work."

Just as childbirth is a very personal matter, with varying degrees of pain and suffering, so too is spiritual travail a very personal matter. My experiences might differ from yours, but the end result is the same. Just as an experienced mother imparts advice to those young mothers who are about to give birth to their first child, I also want to pass on to you a few of my experiences of travail, so that you can identify some of the signs that might accompany your own spiritual walk.

> SPIRITUAL TRAVAIL IS A VERY PERSONAL MATTER.

One point to make absolutely clear at the very beginning is that spiritual travail is not only for women! There is no gender in spiritual matters.

103

There is neither Jew nor Greek, there is neither slave nor free, there is neither male nor female; for you are all one in Christ Jesus (Galatians 3:28).

Travail, or weeping before the Lord, is a burden in prayer from God, who gives it to whomever He wills—boys, girls, men, or women.

In this chapter, we will look at five different areas concerned with travail. These include:

1. The difference between *burden, travail,* and *warfare.*

2. The Old and New Testament meanings of *travail.*

3. Characteristics of *travail.*

4. The reasons for *travail.*

5. Is everybody supposed to *travail?*

BURDEN, TRAVAIL, AND WARFARE

These three subjects are the source of constant controversy, and yet all have scriptural precedents.

A *burden* is receiving the concern of the Lord, whereas *travail* is the action of bringing that burden to birth and is characterized by weeping, groaning, and pleading.

Many people confuse raw emotionalism with showing emotion before God. Jesus wept at the grave of Lazarus, openly and publicly. However, tears for tears' sake is not a good idea; but when the Holy Spirit begins to move upon you, when He stirs your spirit and you cannot restrain yourself, then this is crying out before God. This is travail; this is crying from your heart in prayer for which sometimes you do not even have the words to speak, but just groan in anguish before Him. This prayer can be so deep and powerful, and yet no word is uttered. This groaning, weeping, or sometimes even silent communication reaches the heart of God.

Once our spirit has received a burden from the Lord, that burden begins to grow, just like a human seed inside the womb of a woman. The growth is cared for and nurtured by prayer and becomes larger and stronger. In time, a visit to the maternity ward is necessary, and travail begins. Remember, a maternity ward is not a mortuary! Life is noisily and messily birthed in one, whereas the other only sees death and clinical orderliness. Travail brings the burden of the Lord to fruition.

TRAVAIL BRINGS THE
BURDEN OF THE
LORD TO FRUITION.

Sometimes, the birth of a child becomes complicated. The same can happen in the spiritual realm, and that is when the Holy Spirit comes and gives utterances that we cannot express.

> *Likewise the Spirit also helps in our weaknesses. For we do not know what we should pray for as we ought, but the Spirit Himself makes intercession for us **with groanings which cannot be uttered** (Romans 8:26).*

While travail is the action of bringing the burden to birth, warfare is the action of protecting that burden from the assaults of the enemy.

In the first chapter, we referred to the Hebrew word paga and its various meanings—to collide, to encroach upon, to drive in, to strike up against, to be violent against; and from those meanings, we derive the following definitions:

Travail—*facing* the Father, on behalf of a person or situation (the burden), through weeping, prayer, and pleading for that person or situation (burden). This represents one edge of the double-edged sword.

Warfare—*facing* satan or the oppressive forces, in the name of Jesus, on behalf of a person, or a situation (the burden). This represents the opposite edge of the sword.

So we see the two actions of the word *paga* again, and God will use both. However, in God, there is balance. It is not all warfare, neither is it all travail; it is a combination of both. And in the midst of it all, there is the wonderful presence of worship.

As mentioned in Chapter 1, think of *paga* as a two-edged sword, with its two edges of *travail* and *warfare* held together by the hilt—worship. Having considered spiritual warfare in Chapters 3 and 4, we will now concentrate on *travail*, or to give it another name—the prayer of compassion.

The word "compassion" is derived from the Latin word *com-pati*, which means a deep feeling of joining your heart with the heart of a person, or that which God has laid upon your heart (the burden). The "com" part of "compassion" means "together."

When we pray, we are never alone; we are partners with Jesus, by the Holy Spirit.

> For through Him [Jesus] we both have access by one Spirit to the Father (Ephesians 2:18).

So, when we come to this word "com," meaning "together" and the word "pati," which means to suffer or endure, then we are suffering with, or enduring with whatever has caused that compassion. Your pain is my pain. We see this evident in Psalm 23.

> Yea, though I walk through the valley of the shadow of death, I will fear no evil; for You are with me; Your rod and Your staff, they **comfort** me (Psalm 23:4).

Here, the word "comfort" in the Hebrew is nacham, which means to comfort, to console.

This repetition of meaning is important, in order to bring a full understanding of what it really means to travail, to pray the prayers of compassion. It is not a polite nod of the head, indicating that you have seen someone's dire situation, and that, while you feel sorry for them, you are unable to do anything about resolving the issue.

Travail signifies weeping with those who are weeping, sighing with those who are sighing, and entering into the conflict yourself, because they are unable to do so.

Jesus did exactly that. He entered the conflict because we were unable to do so.

Maybe you have never experienced it, or you might say, "I am simply not sensitive enough." Then start praying for it. Ask the Lord to let you feel the way He feels about matters. Ask Him to let you see with His eyes, and very soon you will have no problem with empathy. I think there is no prayer I pray more often than this: "Lord, let me feel the way You feel." This is especially helpful when you do not have a burden for the lost or when you pray for those who might irritate and frustrate you. Let me share with you one experience I had.

I happened to be severely criticized by a pastor who worked in the group where I ministered at that time. For four years, this man made my life impossible. He even vowed that he would not rest until I was off the team; needless to say, this caused severe tension within the team and especially for me. I fasted, prayed, forgave, rebuked. I did everything I knew, and yet my heart was not free, until one day, I realized that my constant complaining about him was simply joining "the accuser of the brethren" (see Rev. 12:10). God knew about him already, and my complaints did not change anything. Then I prayed, "Lord, show me the way that You see him." The deepest travail suddenly came upon me. I wept for his ministry, his family, his call in God; tremendous compassion went through me. Once it lifted, I said, "Lord, is that how You feel about him?" Of course, it was how God felt about him, and it was a lesson that I have never forgotten. Soon the breakthrough came. God moved him on to different mission fields, and we became good working colleagues.

THE BIBLICAL MEANING OF TRAVAIL

Once again, it is the significance of the words in the original language that is so important for a correct understanding of the Bible.

> *Now it came to pass, at the time for **giving birth** [travail], that behold, twins were in her womb* (Genesis 38:27).

In Hebrew, "travail" is *yalad* and is used nearly five hundred times, meaning, to bare, bring forth, travail, to be a midwife.

Sometimes, traveling in Israel was likened to travail, so difficult was the journey.

> *And Moses told his father-in-law all that the Lord had done to Pharaoh and to the Egyptians for Israel's sake, all the **hardship** [travail] that had come upon them on the way, and how the Lord had delivered them* (Exodus 18:8).

The word for "hardship" (*telaah* in Hebrew) also means trouble, or travail.

For a further example of how travail can be pictured, consider the following:

*He shall see the **labor** [travail] of His soul, and be satisfied. By His knowledge My righteous Servant shall justify many, for He shall bear their iniquities* (Isaiah 53:11).

This word (*amal* in Hebrew) means labor, toil, trouble, and many other lesser meanings. Its sense can be seen in the following verse:

*Then we cried out to the Lord God of our fathers, and the Lord heard our voice and looked on our affliction and our **labor** [amal] and our oppression* (Deuteronomy 26:7).

Finally, the child-bearing meaning of travail is found in Jeremiah:

*For I have heard a voice as of a woman in **labor** [travail], the anguish as of her who brings forth her first child, the voice of the daughter of Zion bewailing herself* (Jeremiah 4:31a).

This final version of "travail" is *chalah* in Hebrew, and means to be grieved, to pray, to be wounded.

All these various meanings give some depth and color to the understanding of what it means to travail.

In the New Testament, this subject is also very well covered in the Greek.

*My little children, for whom I **labor in birth** [odino] again until Christ is formed in you* (Galatians 4:19).

Odino means to feel the pains of childbirth, and this is true travail. Also, in Romans, there is a similar passage.

*For we know that the whole creation groans and **labors with birth pangs together** until now* (Romans 8:22).

This idea of "labors with birth pangs together" (*sunodino*) means to undergo agony (like a woman in childbirth) "together with." We have seen this concept of "together with" in the first chapter.

Our best example is always the Lord Jesus Christ, and He certainly *travailed.*

*Who, in the days of His flesh, when He had offered up **prayers and supplications, with vehement cries and tears** to Him who was able to save Him from death, and was heard because of His godly fear* (Hebrews 5:7).

Therefore, when Jesus saw her weeping, and the Jews who came with her weeping, He **groaned in the spirit and was troubled** (John 11:33).

This brief Hebrew and Greek lesson hopefully helps provide you with a better understanding of the word *travail* in the Word of God.

CHARACTERISTICS OF TRAVAIL

1. *Travail is from the Holy Spirit.*

   Travail is not something that can be switched on and off like a light bulb or put on and off like a coat. Travail comes from the Holy Spirit and flows out of worship. If it does not come from the Holy Spirit, then it is only of the flesh, and nothing is birthed, no matter how spiritual the settings, how glorious the sounds, or how wonderful you feel.

   Moreover, neither does travail happen every time that you pray. Just as you can walk in and out of a maternity ward without producing a baby, so you can pray without travail. But, once you are pregnant with a burden, then travail will happen sooner or later, and the maternity ward will be required!

2. *Times and tears.*

   Many times, I have found myself crying. Now, I am not the kind of woman who cries because it is a good idea, but it is a different story when the Spirit of the Lord moves upon me.

   Once, I found myself crying for almost two weeks. Every time I prayed, I just cried and cried. Nobody else knew about it. It was between the Lord and me. But for all this crying, I had no idea why I was crying. I did not have a special burden; I did not even know what that Lord wanted with it. But one thing I did know—I knew not to stop! I also knew that in due course, when the time of travail was over, the Lord would explain what it was all about and stop it.

   About two weeks later, I attended a Christian camp, at which the Lord brought many to salvation, and signs and wonders were in great evidence. I knew then that these tears of travail birthed what had happened at that camp.

3. *The Holy Spirit does not offend.*

    Intercessors do not draw attention to themselves. They use wisdom as to where and when to travail. During the preaching of the Word of God is not the time to howl and weep in travail. Wisdom dictates the time and place for such actions.

    However, practically, what are you to do if, during a meeting, travail comes upon you strongly? Simply leave the meeting, go outside, sit in the car, or on a bench, and pray. There, no one else in that meeting will be disturbed, and your travail can be continued between God and yourself. Once the burden has lifted, you can return to the meeting without anyone else being the wiser for your absence.

    Many times, when there was no other place of privacy, I simply went to the ladies' room, closed the door, and prayed. The people outside had no idea of what was happening, but the spirit world certainly took note.

    Travail prayers do not have to be loud or excessive. "It is not by might, nor by power, but by My Spirit," says the Lord of hosts.

    An intercessor does not have a "higher spirituality" than the rest of the Body of Christ, if he or she travails. We are all part of one body, with Christ as the head. Therefore, wisdom and sensitivity are required. Sadly, I have noticed how some intercessors suddenly go into travail when leaders are around. That happened, for example, when I and some of the leaders prayed together before a meeting. One sister went into travail that was so loud and overpowering, it distracted everybody during the prayer time. I cut the prayer time short and said, "Leave her and let us go. The Lord Himself is quite capable of bringing this burden to birth." Three seconds after we left the room, the lady was right next to us again. Was that travail really from the Spirit? I certainly doubt it.

The flow of the Holy Spirit can be long or short. Travail can come quickly, and the burden lift again just as quickly, once the Spirit has done what He wants to do.

Once, I sat working on my computer in a hotel room with the window open. Many emergency vehicles with their sirens came and went without them drawing my attention. Suddenly, an ambulance came past again. The moment I heard that siren, a tremendous burden hit my heart. I fell on my knees and started to pray, crying out for the life in danger. Travail poured through my spirit. After about five minutes it lifted, and I knew that the job was done. The life in the ambulance would be saved from death. I never knew who it was, but I will certainly meet that person in Heaven.

4. *Peace follows the lifting of the burden.*

How do you know when the travail is over? How do you know when a baby is born? There is a peace that follows the birth. It can appear as a quietness in the spirit or great joy; it can seem as a complete rest in the Lord or simply as a release from a burden.

You might not know why you are travailing or what the purpose of that travail is; nevertheless, you will know when it has passed.

REASONS FOR TRAVAIL

There are at least seven reasons for travail, listed as follows:

1. *The primary reason is the lost.*

   Rivers of water *run down from my eyes, because men do not keep Your law* (Psalm 119:136).

   Consider what the psalmist is actually saying in this verse—rivers of tears flow down my cheeks, because Your law is not obeyed. In other words, "Lord, I am weeping, because of the lost and damned."

2. *Identification with the sin and the needs.*

So often, God has me weeping over the current state of my home nation, Germany, and the sin, degradation, and hopelessness of the lives of our citizens. Sometimes, together with like-minded friends, we cry out for our government. In these situations, we find that the Holy Spirit encourages us to identify with a situation, so that we can bring it in prayer before the throne of Almighty God. It becomes a more intimate, personal petition, than if you simply read about a situation in the daily newspaper.

> *The Lord said to him, "Go through the midst of the city, through the midst of Jerusalem, and put a mark on the foreheads of the men who **sigh and cry** over all the abominations that are done within it"* (Ezekiel 9:4).

Here, the angel was to look for, and mark, those who cried over the current moral, political, and religious state of the city of Jerusalem.

3. *Deliverance.*

> *I have surely seen the oppression of My people who are in Egypt; **I have heard their groaning** and have come down to deliver them. And now come, I will send you to Egypt* (Acts 7:34).

Has it ever occurred to you that God sent you to the city where you live because He had heard the cry of the people in that city? Has it ever occurred to you that you were sent with a purpose because God was looking for a man or a woman whom He could send to that place, because He had heard their groaning? He has heard the cry of the streets, the cry of the bordellos, and He has seen the sin before Him. He hears the cry of the lonely, the cry of the brokenhearted, the cry of the widows, and the cry of the fatherless. They all are in our cities.

GOD SENT YOU TO YOUR CITY BECAUSE HE HAD HEARD THE CRY OF THE PEOPLE IN THAT CITY.

We may not be sent to Egypt, but we are certainly sent to the spiritual Egypts. That is the whole plan and purpose of God.

4. *Repentance and growth in the Church.*

    *My little children, for whom I **labor in birth again** until Christ is formed in you* (Galatians 4:19).

    *Thus says the Lord of hosts: "Consider and call for the **mourning** women, that they may come; and send for skillful **wailing** women, that they may come. Let them make haste and take up a **wailing** for us, that **our eyes may run with tears, and our eyelids gush with water.** For a voice of wailing is heard from Zion: 'How we are plundered! We are greatly ashamed, because we have forsaken the land, because we have been cast out of our dwellings.'" Yet hear the word of the Lord, O women, and let your ear receive the word of His mouth; teach your daughters **wailing**, and everyone her neighbor a lamentation* (Jeremiah 9:17-20).

    *I have not come to call the righteous, but sinners, to **repentance*** (Luke 5:32).

5. *Spiritual breakthrough.*

    *"Who has heard such a thing? Who has seen such things? Shall the earth be made to give birth in one day? Or shall a nation be born at once? For as soon as Zion was in labor, she gave birth to her children. **Shall I bring to the time of birth, and not cause delivery?**" says the Lord. "Shall I who cause delivery shut up the womb?" says your God* (Isaiah 66:8-9).

6. *Fulfillment of prophecy.*

    Then Elijah said to Ahab, "Go up, eat and drink; for there is the sound of abundance of rain." So Ahab went up to eat and drink. And Elijah went up to the top of Carmel; then he bowed down on the ground, and put his face between his knees, and said to his servant, "Go up now, look toward the sea." So he went up and looked, and said, "There is nothing." And seven times he said, "Go again." Then it came to pass the seventh time, that he said, "There is a cloud, as small as a man's hand, rising out of the sea!" (1 Kings 18:41-44a)

In these verses, we can see that God uses travail to bring into existence the fulfillment of the prophetic word. Although fire fell on Carmel, it was not fire that was promised, but rain! Thus, Elijah brought the promise of God to fruition through travail.

7. *The nations.*

> *Ask of Me, and I will give You* **the nations** *for Your inheritance, and the ends of the earth for Your possession* (Psalm 2:8).

IS EVERYONE SUPPOSED TO TRAVAIL?

The very short answer is...*no*. Travail is a prerogative of the Holy Spirit. Each aspect of prayer—worship, travail, warfare—is as important as the other, and as we all are parts of one body, the Holy Spirit uses whomever is available or whom He chooses to meet the demand of the moment.

It has happened to me that sometimes, God had me pray for something for a long time, and then used somebody else to bring it to birth! At first, I did not really understand that. I did the hard work—carrying the burden over months, in fasting and prayer—and then suddenly, somebody else was His instrument for solving the problem. As I sought the Lord about this matter, He said, "You are one body, and through My body, I build My Kingdom." I went back and looked at my motives. Was I doing what I was doing only for Jesus, so that He received the glory? I found room for pride in my life and had to repent.

How should I pray when in travail?

- You can pray in the spirit (tongues).
- You can pray with your understanding (your own language).
- You can weep without any specific praying.
- You can pray loudly, quietly, or silently.
- You can pray with a deep inner groaning or sorrow too heavy to express.

CHAPTER 7

A Burden and How to Pray It Through

A BURDEN IS FEELING THAT which God Himself is feeling, and like prayer, it comes to us via Jesus, by His Holy Spirit into our hearts. We then return that to Almighty God by the Holy Spirit through Jesus and thus to the Father, whereupon God answers the prayer, or in other words, resolves the burden.

From God the Father

to God the Father

via Jesus

via Jesus

by His Holy Spirit

by His Holy Spirit

to us

From us

BURDENS DIFFER
FROM PERSON TO
PERSON, AND EACH
BURDEN IS UNIQUE
TO THAT PERSON.

Burdens differ from person to person, and each burden is unique to that person. Your pastor or your spouse might not understand your feelings, just as you cannot understand some of theirs. However, you must do what God has given you to do, allow me to do what God has given me to do, and permit others to do the things that God wants them to do. That way, the full purpose of God is achieved.

I have found that throughout my life as an intercessor, burdens come in two different ways, which I describe as an *impulse burden* and a *long-term burden*.

THE IMPULSE BURDEN

One of my specialities as a registered nurse (before I became a missionary) was that of emergency nursing. No matter what I was doing—writing a report, caring for a patient, or having a cup of tea—as soon as the emergency signal sounded, I dropped everything in order to deal with that emergency. Why? Because it was a matter of life or death. I stayed at the emergency post until the situation was resolved or until another department took over.

The impulse burden is the emergency call of the Holy Spirit. Now obviously, God does not need puny man to come to His rescue, but in His wonderful love for us, He has involved His children in what He is doing. Just as a human father involves his young son in some of the easier aspects of the family business, in order to teach him and show him what to do, and also because he loves to have his son work together with him, so too does our heavenly Father involve us in His work. Neither father needs the help of the child. In fact, sometimes, it creates more problems than it solves, but because of the love of the father for the offspring, that love triumphs. The problems can always be solved later!

The impulse burden, in true emergency style, demands immediate attention and immediate obedience. It calls for the highest form of sensitivity to God. It is not enough to receive the call; instant action is what saves the day.

Imagine the scene again in the hospital, when the emergency signal sounds. I receive the call, but unless I act upon that call, I cannot deal

with the emergency. The same applies to
the impulse burden. It is no good to simply be aware that you have received a burden from Almighty God. Unless you act
upon that burden immediately, then
nothing will happen. It is no use thinking
to yourself, *Ah, yes, I have a crashing burden from the Lord for so-and-so. I will pray*

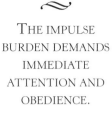

THE IMPULSE
BURDEN DEMANDS
IMMEDIATE
ATTENTION AND
OBEDIENCE.

*about that when I get home this evening. Meanwhile, I have to do the
shopping.* That is no good at all! The Holy Spirit is allowing you to feel
the heart of God at that moment for a particular person or a specific
situation, and it needs prompt attention.

Now, many people say to me, "It's all right for you, Suzette—you're
a full-time intercessor, and you have all day to pray!" How wrong can
some people be? Many times, I have been at a meal with leaders and
pastors, when suddenly this impulse burden and urge to pray comes
upon me. I simply excuse myself from the table, walk into the ladies'
room, and pray! I then return to the table, and rejoin the conversation,
with no one being any the wiser as to what has happened between my
Father and me. But in the spirit realm, the Father knew and the devil
knew that I happened to be in partnership with my Father concerning
that situation, even though it took only a minute or two.

Often, I hear something, and know immediately that I should pray
about it. For instance, as I mentioned in the previous chapter, I was once
in a hotel room, busy working on my laptop, when the sound of a siren
floated through the open window. The very second I heard the siren,
something hit my spirit—it was the call of God to pray. Now, whenever
an ambulance passes me, or I see an accident, I immediately start praying for the people involved. Because I have a constant relationship with
my heavenly Father—not only when I am on my knees, or in my quiet
time, but even while at work—I can recognize His call to action.

In Him we live and move and have our being (Acts 17:28a).

If I type on my computer, I am in Him. If I go shopping, I am in
Him. We are in Him all the time and therefore, we can receive the impulse burden at any time of day or night! We serve an omniscient God.
Therefore, when the impulse burden comes, He is fully aware of your
situation and capabilities. He is your Father and will not ask you to do

the impossible! He will not insist that you spend three hours in solid prayer if He knows that you have an appointment in two hours. He is the God of order!

Following are a few scriptural examples of an impulse burden:

> *Therefore, when Jesus saw her weeping, and the Jews who came with her weeping, He **groaned in the spirit and was troubled**. And He said, "Where have you laid him?" They said to Him, "Lord, come and see." Jesus **wept*** (John 11:33-35).

> *Now as He drew near, He saw the city and **wept** over it* (Luke 19:41).

> *So it was, when the Angel of the Lord spoke these words to all the children of Israel, that the people **lifted up their voices and wept*** (Judges 2:4).

> *But many of the priests and Levites and heads of the fathers' houses, old men who had seen the first temple, **wept with a loud voice** when the foundation of this temple was laid before their eyes. Yet many shouted aloud for joy* (Ezra 3:12).

Before finishing this subject, I want to give you a practical illustration of how I came to better understand an impulse burden. This example will show you just how important it is to listen to the Holy Spirit and to obey His promptings.

I had finished preaching at a large conference, and was praying for the sick, when a lady came onto the platform from the side. She approached me, gently took my hand, and said, "Suzette, would you please pray for my husband *now*?" Signs and wonders were already being seen in the auditorium, yet this lady wanted me to pray for her husband right away. Normally, I would pass the person to one of the platform staff to deal with, but as soon as she took hold of my hand, the Spirit of God spoke to my heart, and said, "Her husband is going to commit suicide, *now*!"

What do you do in these circumstances? I could not tell her what the Holy Spirit had just revealed to me, and I was still wondering if I had heard correctly. As I looked around, the burden of God came upon me, and I knew that the man was going to die.

I turned to the leaders and said, "Please excuse me, but we really need to pray into a situation, right now." The pastor said that that was fine, so I encouraged the musicians to play softly and asked the congregation to remain in worship and prayer. And that is what they did. They prayed, worshipped, and prayed some more; but the burden of God continued to lay heavy on my heart. I prayed and prayed and prayed. Had I not been the guest speaker and still on the stage with the microphone, I would have gone to some quiet area to pour out my prayers to the Lord. However, I could not leave, so I continued praying, and the people prayed with me.

Ten minutes turned to fifteen, and still no breakthrough. The pastor came and said that he thought we should move on, as time was quickly passing. "Trust me," I said. "Let's continue to pray some more."

Shortly after that, the burden just lifted from my heart, and I felt at peace. I looked at the lady and said to her, "Go home, and tomorrow, come and tell us what has happened."

The next day, the lady returned and related the following story.

"Last night," she said, "I went home and waited for my husband. I waited and waited. Finally, around two o'clock, he came in, sat on my bed, and said, 'You know that we have such great problems in our life, financially as well as in our marriage. Well, last night, I decided to kill myself. I took my revolver, and went out in the car into the countryside. I was going to blow my brains away. I loaded the gun, put it to my head, and at that moment, I looked at my watch and said, "O God." I just cried to God, and then I pulled the trigger. It didn't go off, so I pointed it out the car window, and pulled the trigger again. Bang! It went off. I loaded it again, put the muzzle into my mouth, and pulled the trigger once again. Click. I tried again. Click. Then I realized that God was doing something in my life. I got out of the car, fell on my knees and gave my life to Jesus Christ.'"

The lady asked him what time it was that this had happened. Yes, it was at the very same time we had been praying!

This story is an example of an impulse burden related to an emergency situation. It does not always have to be that dramatic. But every time the Holy Spirit trusts you by burdening your heart, you must know that it is important to God, no matter how great or small the situation might be in your eyes.

THE LONG-TERM BURDEN

As the name suggests, the long-term burden is one for which we pray about constantly. Examples of long-term burdens would be your city, your church, your neighborhood, and your unsaved family.

Praying for long-term burdens is like building a spiritual highway through the wastelands—it takes time, effort, and persistence in order to see the project completed.

> *Go through, go through the gates! Prepare the way for the people; build up, build up the highway! Take out the stones, lift up a banner for the peoples!* (Isaiah 62:10)

These are commands, and not mere suggestions from the Lord—"*Go* through the gates! *Prepare* the way! *Build* up the highway! *Take* out...*Lift* up!"

Likewise, *intercession, as well as evangelism, are not suggestions—they are commands.*

Paul knew something about long-term burdens when he wrote to the Galatians—a passage that we have looked at before.

> *My little children, for whom I labor in birth **again** until Christ is formed in you* (Galatians 4:19).

He continually prayed and cared for the churches. Moreover, in the famous passage dealing with his beatings and perilous journeys, he ends with the statement:

> *Besides the other things, what comes upon me daily: **my deep concern for all the churches*** (2 Corinthians 11:28).

Daily, he was concerned about and cared for the churches. Although he could obviously be physically present only in one area at a time, still he was in constant prayer and travail for those in other areas. Consider the next Scripture:

> *It shall come to pass in that day that his burden will be taken away from your shoulder, and his yoke from your neck, and the yoke will be destroyed because of the anointing oil* (Isaiah 10:27).

Ask yourself, "What is it that will be taken away in that day?" It is the burden! His burden will be taken away from your shoulder.

As we travail for the burden given to us by the Holy Spirit, we take, as it were, that burden upon ourselves. We become yoked together with the one suffering, and we share in the pain and suffering. This is true compassion—feeling for others and doing something about their situation. This yoke that is now on both of you is destroyed because of your anointing as you prayed.

It is like a pair of oxen yoked together by a farmer in order to plow a field. Both pull the plow together, sharing in the burden of the work. Then at the end of the day, the yoke is removed, and the two beasts are freed from their toil.

TUNING INTO YOUR SPIRITUAL ANTENNA

As born-again believers in the Lord Jesus Christ, we are a spirit being living in a human body. We have a spirit, soul, and body.

> *Now may the God of peace Himself sanctify you completely; and may your whole **spirit, soul, and body** be preserved blameless at the coming of our Lord Jesus Christ* (1 Thessalonians 5:23).

The body is the outward physical being; the soul comprises the mind, the will, and the emotions; and the spirit is that which has been made alive in Christ.

> *For as in Adam all die, even so in Christ all shall be **made alive*** (1 Corinthians 15:22).

> *And you, being dead in your trespasses and the uncircumcision of your flesh, He has **made alive** together with Him, having forgiven you all trespasses* (Colossians 2:13).

Your spirit can be likened, for the sake of analogy, to a television antenna. In this modern world, television waves are all around us. We cannot see them, feel them, or hear them. We are not aware of their presence, yet even so, they pass through our homes and our offices. And so it is with the state of your spirit before it was made alive in Christ. The spirit realm was all around, but you could not perceive it in spirit and in truth.

However, once you are made alive in Christ, your spirit is like that TV antenna. When you acquire a television and an antenna, television waves are soon visible on the screen of the TV. Likewise, your spirit picks up all sorts of "radiation" from the spirit realm, and you can receive either good or bad programs, just as in the natural. Tune into the good, and tune out the evil.

During the day, I am very busy with meetings, traveling and so on; therefore, the Holy Spirit usually speaks to me at night or very early in the morning. Sometimes He comes and reveals circumstances or matters through my dreams, what is actually happening in the spirit realm over that city or area. Now, it is vitally important that you do not come under condemnation or take these principles out of context. God is a God of balance, and it is more important to worship Him than to be concerned about demonic spirits, or whether you discern correctly or not—then He will lead you into discernment. Walk with joy in the light you have and God will lead you further. None of us are yet perfect, but if we walk in faith, in purity, and in the light, we are in Him. He will guide us!

> But if we walk in the light as He is in the light, we have fellowship with one another, and the blood of Jesus Christ His Son cleanses us from all sin (1 John 1:7).

I found myself having dreams, which were not clean. It greatly concerned me, as I do not feed my spirit on worldly, unclean movies and other types of programs or material. Moreover, it brought me under condemnation. Subsequently, during a time of fasting and prayer, the Lord revealed to me that it had nothing to do with me as a person. I soon began to realize that these dreams were in fact God's way of showing me what kind of spiritual problems or demonic attacks were being inflicted upon that city. I learned to take that and to start praying about it.

Once, while I was in Argentina, known for its wonderful family relationships, I dreamed only about incest for two or three nights! I began to pray, and decided that we would confront the issue head-on.

At the next meeting, I started addressing the subject through a word of knowledge and through discernment. We had people kneeling and weeping everywhere. Both young and old said that they had been affected by incest and the like. God had showed me in my dreams, by His Spirit (through the spiritual antenna, as it were), what was going on.

If you are not feeding your spirit on the worldly rubbish that is available, then this type of message must be coming from the Holy Spirit, as a long-term burden for you to pray into and seek a solution.

On another occasion, I was sitting in my office, working away and feeling fine. I had been having no problems; the ministry was going well, and I was working steadily. Suddenly, I felt such a heaviness descend upon me. On my way home, I asked the Lord whose burden had fallen on my shoulders, whose yoke was on my feelings, as I had no reason in the natural to feel so discouraged. Immediately, the name of a very close missionary friend came to me. I had spoken to her only a few hours before, and she had not mentioned that anything was wrong. Later, I realized that because we are spirit-beings, I had picked up her burden. Because we are partners with Christ, He burdens us with what moves Him. My friend had been greatly discouraged and over-burdened at that time, although she had not mentioned it over the phone.

The sudden realization that my "spiritual antenna" was picking up her burden, and it launched me into prayer for her. I went home, put on a worship CD, and started to worship. I knew that if I prayed, the anointing in prayer would break that yoke. The moment that yoke was broken over me, the burden was released over her, and that is exactly what happened in the spirit realm. I had a choice—I could have tried to sleep off my depression, which is something that so many people do, or I could pray! Trying to sleep off a burden will only make you feel dull when you wake up. On the other hand, ten minutes of active prayer will do more for your spirit in this situation than an hour of sleep. Try it—it is exciting!

TRYING TO SLEEP OFF A BURDEN WILL ONLY MAKE YOU FEEL DULL WHEN YOU WAKE UP.

The main issue is not if you actually have a burden for someone, and who or what you are discerning. Rather, if there is a heaviness upon you, you have to get your spirit free—discernment or no discernment, you need to get back in victory! If you have picked up a person, a word, or a thing, then your victory will set yourself, as well as the person your spirit might have picked up, free! I always say, "It is not so important what we see or discern in the spirit, but what we do with what we see or discern." I compare discernment and the long-term burden to a camera with a wide-angle lens. At first, you have a very wide and even a vague picture, but as you start praying about it, the picture becomes sharper, and soon the Holy Spirit focuses on a specific area. Start praying about that.

Pray Your Promises Into Being

Finally, you *must* pray your promises into being. Elijah had to pray the rain into being.

> *So Ahab went up to eat and drink. And Elijah went up to the top of Carmel; then he bowed down on the ground, and put his face between his knees, and said to his servant, "Go up now, look toward the sea." So he went up and looked, and said, "There is nothing." And seven times he said, "Go again." Then it came to pass the seventh time, that he said, "There is a cloud, as small as a man's hand, rising out of the sea!" So he said, "Go up, say to Ahab, 'Prepare your chariot, and go down before the rain stops you.'" Now it happened in the meantime that the sky became black with clouds and wind, and **there was a heavy rain**. So Ahab rode away and went to Jezreel* (1 Kings 18:42-45).

It is futile just to sit and wait. Promises and burdens must be prayed about. Follow the example of the apostles, who prayed after Peter and John were released from jail.

> *"Now, Lord, look on their threats, and grant to Your servants that with all boldness they may speak Your word, by stretching out Your hand to heal, and that signs and wonders may be done through the name of Your holy Servant Jesus." And **when they had prayed**, the place where they were assembled together was shaken; and they were all filled with the Holy Spirit, and they spoke the word of God with boldness* (Acts 4:29-31).

Refresh Your Spirit

Pray until a breakthrough comes, no matter how long it takes. If you feel that you have prayed through, but do not see the manifestation, then simply continue bringing the matter before God in worship and thanksgiving.

It is extremely important to return to worship after you have prayed. The long-term or short-term burden can be extremely demanding, so the best way to refresh your spirit is to return to worship.

CHAPTER 8

The Birthing of a Vision

MANY OF US HAVE A vision in our heart that we do not know what to do with. Yet in the meantime, simply waiting for something to happen will not produce anything. Remember, your vision will always look too big for you to handle. Moreover, if you can achieve it purely by your gifting, I doubt that the vision is from God, for true vision demands faith, as we will discuss later. God lays a vision in our hearts the way He sees it and how He wants us to develop personally, for He speaks of those things that are not as though they are! If you look at your own abilities, you will never achieve the vision laid on your heart; but in Christ, you can do all things. The purpose of this chapter is to teach you how to pray that vision into existence.

A PERSONAL VISION BROUGHT FORTH BY PRAYER

Where there is no vision, the people perish (Proverbs 29:18a KJV).

The Lord always gives His children something special for which they are responsible to grow and expend their gifts and ministry on. For some, it might be a vision for orphans; for others, perhaps it is a vision for teaching the Word of God to those in impoverished situations. God places

YOUR VISION
WILL ALWAYS
LOOK TOO BIG
FOR YOU
TO HANDLE.

something into each person's heart; and what He puts there is not necessarily for the whole world to join, but just for you and perhaps a select few. That is the great beauty of our Father—He gives us different burdens and visions because He purposes to work through us in that specific area.

Before we go any further though, let me define what is meant by *vision* in this context. It is not a picture that you see in front of your eyes, whether they are open or closed. Examples of those who had this type of vision are Paul, Ezekiel, and Daniel. A second type of vision is the impression of something on your spirit, through which the Lord wants to communicate to you.

However, the vision that we are concerned with is something that has been planted in your heart and is developing as a long-term burden. It is something whereby He can bring forth His divine plan and purpose in a specific area. This type of vision has to be prayed into existence.

In order to bring forth whatever has been laid on your spirit by the Lord, you must come once again into the circle of prayer. True prayer starts in the heart of the Father, comes via Jesus, by His Spirit into our hearts. We now come before the Father and together with the intercession of Jesus and the Holy Spirit, we bring this matter before Him; the Father responds by answering the prayer.

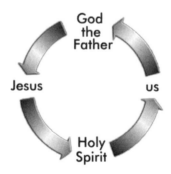

FAITH

In any vision, there has to be faith—rock-solid, unwavering, concrete faith! It is not the size of your faith, but the *strength* of your faith that matters. Faith that is only the size of a mustard seed will do just fine; a mustard seed is a solid, composite entity, not a figment of the imagination. Your faith must be grounded and based upon the Word of God, not upon your imagination, or even worse, your presumption.

A walk of faith is a walk of assurance and certainty. When Almighty God has placed a vision upon your heart, and desires that you pray it into fruition, then it is with the greatest assurance and confidence that you may proceed. Now, you might not have all the answers…you might not have any answers; but be assured, God is in complete control of your destiny. And He has not given you a stone instead of bread, nor a scorpion instead of an egg (see Luke 11:11-12).

THE VISION
STARTS WITH
A PASSION IN
YOUR HEART.

The vision starts with a passion in your heart. As you pray, the God-placed desire will increase. You will become focused upon one area, and certain events in your life will combine to form and change you, so that there is clarity in your vision…but it does not happen overnight.

Furthermore, true faith demands boldness and determination. It is pointless having a crystal-clear vision, and not moving out in faith to bring it to fruition. Boldness brings results.

> *Now when they saw the **boldness** of Peter and John, and perceived that they were uneducated and untrained men, they marveled. And they realized that they had been with Jesus* (Acts 4:13).

> *Now, Lord, look on their threats, and grant to Your servants that with all **boldness** they may speak Your word* (Acts 4:29).

If you have an *assurance* in your heart, and you have *clarity* in your heart, and you *know* that this is where your passion lies, and that this is what the Lord has laid within your heart to believe Him for, then your vision is ready to produce results.

Have you ever watched an apple grow on a tree? First the flower and then the bud. You do not pluck that tiny bud off the tree and try to eat it. You leave it to grow. Soon that tiny bud is a huge Bramley cooking apple and ready to be used.

> *For the earth yields crops by itself: first the blade, then the head, after that the full grain in the head* (Mark 4:28).

I remember once going to my spiritual father, Reinhard Bonnke, after many months of prayer and fasting in an attempt to persuade God to use me and asking him why God was not using me the way I wished to be used. He looked at me for a long time without saying a word, as he was waiting to hear from the Lord. After about a minute or two, still looking at me, he said, "Suzette, *the trees of the Lord never grow overnight.*" I have never forgotten it. It became a pillar in my own life, and I have passed it on to thousands and hundreds of thousands of other people—and I am sure it applies to you as well. The trees of the Lord never grow overnight; it is a process.

Moreover, it takes time for the Holy Spirit to deal with us so that we can become supple under His guidance, and when that happens, His purpose in our lives begins to expand. As a child, I grew up on a farm. My father sometimes took the skin of an animal after it had been slaughtered and stretched it over a series of rollers. I used to say to him, "Daddy, it is going to tear." But as an experienced farmer, he knew far more about hide than his young daughter did—and it did not tear. When I was a little older, I asked him what was the purpose of stretching skins, and he said, "At the moment, it is hard and stiff, so I put it on the stretching bank to get it soft and flexible."

Likewise, God sometimes puts us on a spiritual stretching machine to make us soft and flexible. It might seem as though we are about to be torn apart, but the Master knows exactly what He is doing. When we become like clay under the Holy Spirit's care, we are on our way to fulfilling His purpose in our lives.

Abraham learned his lesson well. Paul eulogizes about the faith of Abraham in the following passage.

> *Therefore it is of faith that it might be according to grace, so that the promise might be sure to all the seed, not only to those who are of the law, but also to those who are of the faith of Abraham, who is the father of us all (as it is written, "I have made you a father of many nations") in the presence of Him whom he believed—***God***, who gives life to the dead and* **calls those things which do not exist as though they did***; who, contrary to hope, in hope believed, so that he became the father of many nations, according to what was spoken, "So shall your descendants be"* (Romans 4:16-18).

No unbelief or distrust made him waver (doubtingly question) concerning the promise of God, but he grew strong and was empowered by faith as he gave praise and glory to God (Romans 4:20 AMP).

True faith operates only when you really know in whom you believe. Abraham, who is known as the father of faith, had to learn to believe the Lord, just as we have to learn. It did not come to him quickly and easily; it took time and effort. He had to learn how to act upon that which he believed he had heard from the Lord.

IT IS BETTER TO
WALK ON THE
WATER AND SOME-
TIMES GET WET,
THAN TO SIT IN A
BOAT OF UNBELIEF
AND STAY DRY.

ATTEMPTING TO HELP GOD ALONG

Just like us, Abraham is also known for making mistakes. Peter was a similar type of character. He made many mistakes, but he is the only one (apart from the Lord Jesus) to have walked on water! Remember, It is better to walk on the water and sometimes get wet, than to sit in a boat of unbelief and stay dry. Making mistakes proves that you are at least doing something!

Most of us know the story of Abraham, and how he tried to help God to bring his vision to fruition, by taking a concubine and producing Ishmael. However, the Bible also tells us that Abraham did not waver at the promise of God. God knew Abraham's heart, and although Ishmael was not in the plan of God, when the appointed time had been reached, Abraham and Sarah had Isaac, the one with whom the covenant was to be established.

But My covenant I will establish with Isaac, whom Sarah shall bear to you at this set time next year (Genesis 17:21).

God's plans will not be thwarted by our mistakes. Our blunders might make life difficult for us, but the eternal purposes of Almighty God are unperturbed by these slight deviations. Consider the outcome of Isaac and Ishmael—the covenant was established with the one whom God had already chosen.

God knows what He intends to achieve through your vision. You have to move with God, not try to move God to accommodate your views. He has given you a vision so that you can be empowered by it. That vision, which you delight to contemplate, is given to you so that you can grow strong in faith as you continue to hold it before the Lord in prayer, and watch it develop under His guidance.

Don't Let Your Vision Die

Often that vision lies dormant somewhere or is cast aside as though it were but an impossible dream. When that vision first came, it was like a burning flame. It was incredible. It was wonderful. But with the passage of time, and often not knowing what to do with it, that vision, that flame began to falter and go out. We understand that a fire needs plenty of fuel to keep it alive and burning; otherwise, all that remains of a once mighty fire is a heap of ash. Even the wise virgins took extra oil with them for their lamps, so that the flame would not go out.

The wise took oil in their vessels with their lamps (Matthew 25:4).

So, it might be that all that is left of your once fiery vision is a pile of cold ashes; but under all that ash, there will always be the spark of God's fire. Paul, in effect, told Timothy to fan into flame the gift of God, which is in you.

*Therefore I remind you to **stir up the gift of God** which is in you through the laying on of my hands* (2 Timothy 1:6).

I encourage you—stir up that vision, seek the Lord, confess your apathy about your vision, and in the words of an old song, "Pick yourself up, dust yourself down, and start all over again!"

Why should you do this? Because if you do not do this, then God has to start all over again, training somebody else to fulfill this task. You have been made perfect; your size, experiences, the family you were born in, and all that is about you, good and bad, was preparation for you to do what you need to do. You should invigorate your vision, because it was given to you as God's means of directing your life into the ways and purposes that He has determined for your life.

Visionaries in the Bible

In the Scriptures, there are many people who had a vision that led them to do mighty exploits for their God. Let's review of few of these examples and be reassured to know that there are scriptural precedents for you to follow.

Abraham had a vision.

Then Abram said, "Look, You have given me no offspring; indeed one born in my house is my heir!" And behold, the word of the Lord came to him, saying, "This one shall not be your heir, but one who will come from your own body shall be your heir." Then He brought him outside and said, "Look now toward heaven, and count the stars if you are able to number them." And He said to him, "So shall your descendants be." And he believed in the Lord, and He accounted it to him for righteousness (Genesis 15:3-6).

Joseph had a dream.

Now Jacob dwelt in the land where his father was a stranger, in the land of Canaan. This is the history of Jacob. Joseph, being seventeen years old, was feeding the flock with his brothers. And the lad was with the sons of Bilhah and the sons of Zilpah, his father's wives; and Joseph brought a bad report of them to his father. Now Israel loved Joseph more than all his children, because he was the son of his old age. Also he made him a tunic of many colors. But when his brothers saw that their father loved him more than all his brothers, they hated him and could not speak peaceably to him. Now Joseph had a dream, and he told it to his brothers; and they hated him even more. So he said to them, "Please hear this dream which I have dreamed: There we were, binding sheaves in the field. Then behold, my sheaf arose and also stood upright; and indeed your sheaves stood all around and bowed down to my sheaf." And his brothers said to him, "Shall you indeed reign over us? Or shall you indeed have dominion over us?" So they hated him even more for his dreams and for his words. Then he dreamed still another dream and told it to his brothers, and said, "Look, I have dreamed another dream. And this time, the sun, the moon, and the eleven stars bowed down to me." So he told it to his father and his brothers; and his father rebuked him and said to him, "What is this dream that you have dreamed? Shall your mother and I and your brothers indeed come to bow down to the earth before you?" (Genesis 37:1-10)

Moses had a word.

So He said, "I will certainly be with you. And this shall be a sign to you that I have sent you: When you have brought the people out of Egypt, you shall serve God on this mountain" (Exodus 3:12).

Cornelius had a vision.

About the ninth hour of the day he saw clearly in a vision an angel of God coming in and saying to him, "Cornelius!" (Acts 10:3)

Peter had a vision.

Now while Peter wondered within himself what this vision which he had seen meant, behold, the men who had been sent from Cornelius had made inquiry for Simon's house, and stood before the gate (Acts 10:17).

Paul had a vision.

Therefore, King Agrippa, I was not disobedient to the heavenly vision (Acts 26:19).

Acting on the Promise of God

In order to receive a promise from God, we need to receive a *rhema* Word. The significance of a *rhema* Word was covered in Chapter 5. Financial banks print many thousands of notes; but in order for you to have one, someone must offer it to you, and you must accept it. You cannot print your own money, because that is illegal. Likewise, for a *rhema* Word to be effective, you cannot simply pluck one out of the Bible and make it your own; it has to be offered to you by the Lord. That offering will come to you as a revelation upon a word, phrase, or sentence from the Word of God.

Having received your *rhema* Word, it then has to be confirmed (just to ensure that it was not *you* who decided that it was a good idea to have). If it is from God, He will confirm it again. This confirmation will come through many means, and will be repeated; in addition, you will have an inner witness.

By the mouth of two or three witnesses every word shall be established (2 Corinthians 13:1b).

This confirmation could come from a friend, through a book, from a sermon, or in any way that the Lord considers suitable for you. However, what is of the greatest importance about this confirmation is that it comes out of *revelation*, not information. It is impos-

PROPHETIC UTTER-ANCE IS ONLY FOR CONFIRMATION.

sible to build a life based upon prophetic utterance. Our lives must be built solely on the Word of God.

One further point concerning prophetic utterance—it is only for *confirmation*. No prophetic word is to tell you what to do with your life; it is not directive but solely confirmative.

Most of the time, when the Lord gives a *rhema* Word, it is in what I call "the past tense." By that, I do not imply the strict grammatical usage of the English language. What I mean is that God speaks those things that are not as though they are!

> *God, who gives life to the dead and **calls those things which do not exist as though they did** (Romans 4:17b).*

A biblical example of this "past tense" can be seen in the Book of Joshua.

> *And the Lord said to Joshua: "See!* ***I have given*** *Jericho into your hand, its king, and the mighty men of valor. You shall march around the city, all you men of war; you shall go all around the city once. This you shall do six days" (Joshua 6:2-3).*

The Lord had delivered Jericho, but Joshua and his army still had to do something about it! They had to move, and they had to bring the word into action.

Simply to have the word and have faith that it will happen is not sufficient. We must act in obedience to that word. Another similar example from the Book of Joshua comes two chapters later.

> *Now the Lord said to Joshua: "Do not be afraid, nor be dismayed; take all the people of war with you, and arise, go up to Ai. See,* ***I have given*** *into your hand the king of Ai, his people, his city, and his land" (Joshua 8:1).*

The city of Ai and the land were doomed, but Joshua still had to go and engage in battle for that word to bear fruit.

So, dear child of God, although God has given you the most glorious promises, and spoken to you, and confirmed the word many times, you still need to pray it into being, and take action to ensure that it comes to fulfillment.

I want to give you a personal testimony of how I took action according to a promise given to me by God.

God spoke to me that one day I would preach in the nations, that I would preach in large stadiums, and that I would bring in harvest after harvest.

At first, I never dreamed that this could really happen, until I started preaching to one, then two, and eventually it was five! When I was in charge of a women's work, many times I went into the mountains in Africa to preach the Word. There we were, preaching to three, or four, or five. There were no vast stadiums up there in the mountains. But people were born again, and soon the five grew to ten!

I learned how to preach up there in the mountains with a small congregation, and now I hold my own crusades with hundreds of thousands in a single meeting. Remember, the trees of the Lord never grow overnight.

STEPS TO BRING THE VISION TO BIRTH

Once God has revealed His purpose in your life to you, and has confirmed it again and again, what do you do then? If you want to see any fulfillment of what God has spoken to you, then you must start acting on that vision in small ways, just as I did.

1. *Pray your vision and write it down.*

   The first and most important step is to *pray!* Very simply, bring your vision before the Lord in prayer, worship, and fasting. Pray all of the Scriptures that you have been given concerning the vision, over and over to the Lord. Make time daily, for this most important stage.

   The second step is to *write the vision down* so that it becomes clear in your mind and in your spirit. Write it where you can read it daily, where you can keep it in front of your eyes. Why not stick it to your refrigerator with a magnet?

*Then the Lord answered me and said: "**Write the vision and make it plain** on tablets, that he may run who reads it. **For the vision is yet for an appointed time**; but at the end it will speak, and it will not lie. Though it tarries, wait for it; because it will surely come, it will not tarry"* (Habakkuk 2:2-3).

Remember, the vision is yours. Not everybody will understand it, nor necessarily agree with it. However, it is given by God to you!

2. *Realize there is an incubation period—a time of waiting.*

If you are assured that the vision is God ordained, then it will go through an *incubation period*. All seeds, plans, and projects undergo an incubation period, and that includes your vision.

This incubation period is the time when God first speaks the vision, to the time at which it is manifest. It is not a static time; it is an operational period, in which many things take place.

Unfortunately, it is also a period in which many men and women lose what was given to them. Many visions die during this time, or are not encouraged through lack of understanding. It is a time, in which people lose faith, become discouraged, compromise, or lose patience during the waiting.

I strongly want to draw your attention to two vital words that clarify the importance of the waiting or incubation period. Please look again at Habakkuk chapter 2.

*Then the Lord answered me and said: "**Write the vision and make it plain** on tablets, that he may run who reads it. **For the vision is yet for an appointed time**; but at the end it will speak, and it will not lie. Though it tarries, wait for it; because it will surely come, it will not tarry"* (Habakkuk 2:2-3).

The word "tarries" is the Hebrew word *mahahh*. This is a very active word, and implies a reluctant or *active* delay. Faith is never passive, but always active. So, what God is saying is that although there is a delay, active faith should be applied all the time.

The Hebrew word for "wait" in this Scripture is *chakah*. It comes from a word meaning "to pierce through." This is not the implication of the English language in "waiting for something to happen," but it can be compared with a sharp point that pierces through material or an object. This means that while we wait during the incubation period, we need to constantly *chakah* or pierce into the spirit realm by means of active faith (*mahahh*—tarries), until the manifestation of the vision comes into the natural.

Allow me to give you another personal example of this concept of an incubation period.

Although I was working with Reinhard Bonnke, I had not planned to stay with his ministry for long. My vision was to be a courier for Bibles into nations where they were not allowed. One morning during my prayers, the Lord came with a very powerful vision. He said, "I want you to stay with the Reinhard Bonnke ministry, and I want you to lead the intercession." I really thought that I had dreamed that up myself, because it seemed so impossible at that time.

Midmorning the same day, there was a knock at the door. When I opened it, a man said, "My name is Simon Roads. Are you Suzette Hattingh?" I said that I was, and he continued, "I have come 600 kilometers from Zimbabwe [Rhodesia at that time] to tell you that God spoke to me in Zimbabwe, and said, 'Go down to Gaborone [the capital of Botswana] where you will find a crusade of Reinhard Bonnke. There you will find a woman with the name of Suzette Hattingh. Tell her, Thus says the Lord, you are to do the intercession.'"

Being assured of the vision, I went to my spiritual leader, Pastor Bonnke, and shared the happenings with him. Kindly, he told me that he did not have a witness with it at that moment, but that he would pray about it. One month, two months, five months—we both prayed. I thought to myself, *how long will it take before the Lord speaks to him?* But I was not going to rebel against my leader.

Nine months later, Pastor Bonnke called me and told me that God had spoken to him concerning me. "Suzette," he said, "you are to do the intercession!"

Now I was scared. I had prayed for nine months, and now it was finally time to begin a new part of my ministry. In hindsight, I can never thank God enough that Pastor Bonnke did not agree to the intercession when I wanted him to agree. I needed that tarry-and-waiting time to grow in my own spirit, to pierce into the spirit realm, in order to be able to handle it effectively when the right time came. Thank God for spiritual leaders. Remember, it is not your leaders who stop you, for God is the one who is in charge. And just a bit of advice: submission is not restriction, but protection.

This waiting time is really your preparation time. Just as a woman who is pregnant starts to prepare for the new arrival, so also should you begin to prepare through prayer and worship.

3. *Call your vision into existence.*

There is another point that became very vital in my prayer life while praying about the visions God gave me. This is especially important in praying for a nation or specific ministries. Genesis 1:1b says, "*God created the heavens and the earth.*" The word "created" is the word *bara* in Hebrew, which means "to create, to fashion, carving or cutting out." This suggests that creating is similar to sculpturing. When God spoke, "*Let there be light,*" there was light, and that word still has the same creative power even today, because we still have day and night.

Let me put it this way: When God spoke in Genesis chapter 1, that word went out and created and *is still creating!* Once again, Isaiah 55:11 clearly states that God's Word that has gone from His mouth cannot return without fruit or results. Now imagine God's Word in your mouth! It has creative power! For the Spirit of God indwells you. In prayer and worship, we fellowship with the Father, and through us Heaven gets involved in earthly affairs. In absolute humility, worship, and prayer, we can start calling those things that are not as though they are, and sculpt, as it were, things into existence in the spirit realm. Let me give you an example.

One morning God woke me up, and I started praying. He told me to stop asking for revival or a greater flow of the miraculous. He told me to start calling those healings into existence; however, there were no sick people in the room in which I was praying! But I knew about the power to start calling those things that are not as though they are, so that when they stand before me, the piercing or prayer has been done in the spirit realm and the miracle manifests. I have seen that over and over at our crusades. The Lord has me pray for weeks beforehand concerning sicknesses that will be at the crusade, and sometimes, the healing miracles simply start while I am still preaching. God's Word has creative power.

When you pray, what do you give to the Holy Spirit for Him to create with? This is not pride, but partnership; and once again, if you make a mistake, do not be concerned. After all, it is only you and Jesus together in prayer, and the Spirit of God knows the intent of your heart. Start calling your vision into existence, and leave it to the Spirit to change it the way He desires.

4. *Don't attempt to take a detour from God's original plan.*

Sadly, due to the passage of time and growing impatience, Abraham allowed an Ishmael to be born. So often, we too compromise the original vision through pressure of other matters, or we allow people to talk us into something else. Ishmael was not God's promised child; he was Abraham's "good idea." Isaac was the promised child of the vision.

GO BACK TO WHAT THE TRUE VISION OF THE MOST HIGH GOD IS FOR YOU, AND PRAY IT INTO BEING.

Many times, our Ishmaels come in the form of our own programs, or our own ways that we use to help the vision along. That is not the Lord's plan or purpose.

Go back to what God has spoken to you. Go back to what the true vision of the Most High God is for you, and with that, you will be able to keep the sharp, clear picture given by the Holy Spirit, and it will come forth. Though it tarries, do not be dismayed, because at the right time; God will make sure that it comes according to His plans and purposes for your life.

CHAPTER 9

The Song of the Lord

IN THIS CHAPTER, I WANT to share with you some of the practices that I use in my daily prayer life, which have brought me into fresh and new dimensions of prayer.

So often, we separate worship and prayer; however, they are an entity, a whole. In addition, when we talk about the "song of the Lord," please understand that it refers to much more than worship, melody, or prayer.

WORSHIP IS PRAYER AND PRAYER IS WORSHIP

Sometimes your prayer might be with melody; at other times, it can be singing the Psalms to the Lord; and yet at others, it might be the simple song of the Lord flowing out of your spirit, with your own melody, your own words, and your own affections.

WORSHIP IS THE EXPRESSION OF YOUR LOVE BEFORE ALMIGHTY GOD.

Worship is the expression of your love before Almighty God, and revolves around the character of God, whereas praise revolves around what He has done for us. Some people are demonstrative in their love, while others more restrained, but that is no indication of the depth of that love.

HOLY PARTNERS WITH THE LORD

*Therefore, **holy** brethren, **partakers** of the heavenly calling,*
consider the Apostle and High Priest of our confession, Christ
Jesus (Hebrews 3:1).

What is it that makes us holy? We are certainly not holy because we
are good, moral, or philanthropic. We are holy because Jesus Christ died
on the cross of Calvary, so that our sins can be forgiven.

I now want you to consider the word "partaker." In the Greek, it is
metochos, and means "partner, associate, or companion." It is also used
referring to Simon Peter's fishing associates.

*So they signaled to their **partners** in the other boat to come and*
help them (Luke 5:7a).

Again, it is used in relation with Christ and His disciples.

You have loved righteousness and hated lawlessness; therefore
God, Your God, has anointed You with the oil of gladness more
*than Your **companions*** (Hebrews 1:9).

God calls us to be companions or partners with Christ before Him.

*For we have become **partakers** [companions, partners] of*
Christ if we hold the beginning of our confidence steadfast to the
end (Hebrews 3:14).

It is this partnership with Christ that makes us coworkers in whatever we do with Christ, be it worship, praying for the sick, intercession,
or just in stillness before God. It is making God our prayer partner!

HEAVEN WORSHIPS THE GOD WHO IS HERE NOW

I want to invite you to look into Heaven with me, in the Book of
Revelation, the one book that I think describes worship more than any
other book.

John, to the seven churches which are in Asia: Grace to you and
*peace from Him **who is and who was and who is to come,** and*
from the seven Spirits who are before His throne (Revelation 1:4).

*I am the Alpha and the Omega, the Beginning and the End, says the Lord, **who is and who was and who is to come**, the Almighty* (Revelation 1:8).

These were John's own words. He recorded exactly what he had seen and heard. But what did he hear?

Heaven was worshipping, and John was allowed to listen to the response of different heavenly beings in worship. First, John on earth proclaimed to us a truth; then God Himself sealed that truth with His own words; and then we hear the living creatures in worship. And what did they say as they worshipped?

*The four living creatures, each having six wings, were full of eyes around and within. And they do not rest day or night, saying: **"Holy, holy, holy, Lord God Almighty, who was and is and is to come"*** (Revelation 4:8).

Imagine what it must have sounded like as the voices of those holy creatures filled the Heavens with their worship: "Holy, holy, holy..." Those holy creatures were not just repeating "Holy, holy, holy" like parrots. No! Every time they looked upon God, a fresh revelation of the holiness and awesomeness of God broke out upon them, and in absolute reverence they adored the living God, crying out, "Holy, holy, holy!"

While these words were still echoing through Heaven, something else was happening.

*And the twenty-four elders who sat before God on their thrones fell on their faces and worshiped God, saying: "We give You thanks, O Lord God Almighty, the One **who is and who was and who is to come**, because You have taken Your great power and reigned"* (Revelation 11:16-17).

Imagine this picture of worship before the throne. Imagine the moment when the Almighty said, "I am the Alpha and the Omega, the Beginning and the End, who is and who was and who is to come." All the holy beings in Heaven saw a fresh revelation of His holiness and worshiped in ecstatic adoration. Heaven is not a quiet place. (We are told of only one half hour during which there is silence.)

While this worship is occurring, we read about the angel of the waters.

*And I heard the angel of the waters saying: "You are righteous, O Lord, the One **who is and who was and who is to be**, because You have judged these things"* (Revelation 16:5).

Is this not amazing, that when Heaven worships, they all use the same language referring to the Lord God Almighty—*"who is, who was, and who is to come."* John proclaimed it; God sealed it; and the holy beings, the elders, and the angels all used the same terminology. I think Heaven is trying to get a message through to us.

In English, the translations read, "He who was," which is past tense; "He who is," present tense; and "He who is to come," future tense. However, in the Greek, the future tense is not used; rather, it is the present continuous! So it would read like this: "He who was *and is and is continuously coming all the time."* He is the God of the *now.* He is coming this minute. We do not have to wait for something to happen tomorrow. He is the God who was and who is and who is answering your prayer, your need right now. "Today," says the Word of God, "when you hear My voice, ignore it not." Today is the day of salvation. We serve a God of the now; He is coming all the time, like a river that flows continuously, ever flowing.

What Happens When We Worship?

But You are holy, enthroned in the praises of Israel (Psalm 22:3).

The moment we start to worship, the Father is not looking down from Heaven saying to His Son, "Isn't that sweet? That song is inspired by My Spirit." Furthermore, worship is not three fast songs and two slow ones to get the right atmosphere. Remember, worship is the expression of your love in whatever form it might be. The moment that true worship flows from the heart of His children, He comes as your Partner to indwell or be enthroned on that worship.

The verb "enthroned" indicates that wherever God's people exalt His name, He is ready to manifest His Kingdom's power, in the way most appropriate to the situation, as His rule is invited to invade our situation. No matter how simple that worship might sound to you, He comes in His fullness to indwell that worship. For that very reason, I expect signs and wonders to happen while we worship.

Please note, I did not say "while we sing songs," but *"worship."* There is a great difference between singing songs and worshiping in Spirit and in truth, where your heart, soul, body, and entire being is involved in worshipping God, while you might be singing a song. Jesus is the same yesterday, today, and forever. For that very reason, He is not just powerful, or more powerful, or all powerful. There is no variation in Him, which means that He is always at His highest power, and that is the power of the presence that indwells your worship.

When I am worshipping alone in my bedroom, I expect His power to be right where I am; I expect His presence and His Kingdom to fill my prayers as He is enthroned upon that worship. He is my Father, and I am His child.

WHAT HAPPENS IN THE SPIRIT REALM?

Paul, in his second letter to the Corinthians, shows us what happens in the spirit realm when we worship.

> Now **thanks be to God who always leads us in triumph** in *Christ, and through us diffuses the fragrance of His knowledge in every place. For we are to God* **the fragrance of Christ** *among those who are being saved and among those who are perishing* (2 Corinthians 2:14-15).

This letter to the Corinthians was written during the time when Rome was the number-one world superpower. Its legions had traveled far and wide to conquer Rome's enemies and to expand the empire.

When these legions went into battle, they were not equipped with the communications facilities that modern armies have. There were no satellite communications, no secure facilities for headquarters or other divisions, or anything like that. They had to rely upon the simple expedient of banners to convey orders, very much like the navy in Lord Nelson's day used flags hoisted high over the ships to relay commands and instructions. Those who were responsible for the banners were in a very vulnerable position. If the enemy could kill a banner bearer, confusion could reign, at least until another one was in place.

Once the legion had engaged the enemy and had subdued the land, it returned to its garrison for a victory parade in the arena. In the front of the victorious legion rode the commanding general. Behind him came his banner bearers, followed by the legion itself. Behind the legion followed another group of manacled captives.

The whole party moved around the arena, and then the banner bearers laid down the banners, which they had used during the conflict, and picked up wooden poles. These poles had been dipped into very strong spices, which were called "the spices of victory." The tips of these poles were then set alight, and the banner bearers would run through the city, here, there, and everywhere. Remember that these were walled cities, with high walls surrounding and enclosing them. As they ran, the bearers would wave these sticks of victory spices, so that the smell of incense permeated every house and home in the city. When the people smelled the incense, they would set off for the arena, knowing that the army had returned safely.

Hence, the reason that Paul used the words, "the fragrance of Christ." Christ has won the victory, and we run throughout the world waving the "victory spices" of triumph. The moment we begin to worship, the aroma of victory is released into the spirit realm; and just as that aroma filled the whole city, so too does the aroma of your worship fill your room, your house, your street, and your neighborhood. It notifies every demon that its fate is sealed, because Jesus has the victory.

There is another aspect of this fragrance, which is also very important to understand. As the Roman army returned home, the main body of the legion was followed by the manacled captives. These prisoners knew perfectly well that as soon as they smelled those spices, their demise was not far away. Soon, they would be fed to the wild animals, dipped in tar and used as candles, or any one of a multitude of ways of execution at which the Romans were experts. It was the time of their final humiliation.

WHEN WE COMBINE WORSHIP AND PRAYER, GOD INDWELLS THAT PRAYER AND BECOMES OUR PRAYER PARTNER.

The same applies in the spiritual realm. When we worship, that wonderful fragrance of Christ is released, and satan and his demonic hordes are reminded of their eternal humiliation.

The moment that we mix our prayers with worship, it is like a sweet aroma before God. When we combine worship and prayer, God indwells that prayer and becomes our prayer partner.

*When He opened the seventh seal, there was silence in heaven for about half an hour. And I saw the seven angels who stand before God, and to them were given seven trumpets. Then another angel, having a golden censer, came and stood at the altar. He was given much incense, that he should offer it **with the prayers of all the saints** upon the golden altar which was before the throne. And **the smoke of the incense, with the prayers of the saints, ascended before God** from the angel's hand* (Revelation 8:1-4).

Rise up, child of God, rise up in your spirit, raise your voice in worship and prayer. There is no need to go to a physical arena in order to worship, because your worship creates a spiritual arena, where the Captain of the host, Jesus Himself, indwells that worship. And all Heaven is backing you up as you release the fragrance of victory before the Lord, for you are His banner bearer, and your worship is mixed with the spices of victory.

PRAYER IN SONG

In the Word of God, combined prayer and worship is considered a regular practice. Praying through singing was the norm—that was the specific purpose of the Psalms. In the Old Testament, there are several words used in the richness of the Hebrew language in describing praise and worship.

Two words that we will consider are *tephillah* and *tehilla*. Although they both are very powerful words and seem to be similar, they each have their own meaning.

Tephillah is prayer, supplication, intercession, or prayer by means of a song or hymn.

Tehilla means praise, adoration, or thanksgiving to God, in whichever way that is given.

It is the latter word, *tehilla*, that we will consider first.

When King Jehoshaphat was confronted by the armed hordes from the surrounding nations, he put the whole matter into the hands of the Lord, who, through the mouth of a prophet, effectively said, "The battle belongs to the Lord." Early the next morning…

They…went out into the Wilderness of Tekoa; and as they went out, Jehoshaphat stood and said, "Hear me, O Judah and you *inhabitants of Jerusalem: Believe in the Lord your God, and you shall be established; believe His prophets, and you shall prosper." And when he had consulted with the people, he appointed those who should sing to the Lord, and who should praise the beauty of holiness, as they went out before the army and were saying: "Praise the Lord, for His mercy endures forever." Now when they began to sing and **to praise**, the Lord set ambushes against the people of Ammon, Moab, and Mount Seir, who had come against Judah; and they were defeated* (2 Chronicles 20:20-22).

It was the praising of God, extolling His attributes and qualities through singing, that brought the victory.

The psalmist also knew how to come into the presence of the Holy One of Israel.

Enter into His gates with thanksgiving, and into His courts with **praise**. *Be thankful to Him, and bless His name* (Psalm 100:4).

Your spirit functions like a tabernacle, and you are the priest of that tabernacle because your body is the temple of the Holy Ghost. So, you enter into your own tabernacle in your own spirit through praise, just like the tabernacle of old. Go through those gates in your own spirit and heart by means of praise and thanksgiving, and then pour out your heart before Him as the high priest in the Holy of Holies.

TEPHILLAH, OR PRAYER, IS ONE OF THE MOST POWERFUL BIBLI-CAL PRACTICES.

The other word, *tephillah*, or prayer, is one of the most powerful biblical words as far as I am concerned. Singing your own prayer was a normal practice by all people in the Old Testament. Part of King Solomon's prayer during the dedication of the temple was by *tephillah*, and the glory filled the temple.

And the priests could not enter the house of the Lord, because the glory of the Lord had filled the Lord's house (2 Chronicles 7:2).

Then the Lord appeared to Solomon by night, and said to him: "I have heard your **prayer**, *and have chosen this place for Myself as a house of sacrifice"* (2 Chronicles 7:12).

In the New Testament, there are similar types of passages on how to pray by means of song.

*And that the Gentiles might glorify God for His mercy, as it is written: "For this reason I will confess to You among the Gentiles, and **sing to Your name**"* (Romans 15:9).

*What is the conclusion then? I will pray with the spirit, and I will also pray with the understanding. **I will sing with the spirit, and I will also sing with the understanding*** (1 Corinthians 14:15).

*Speaking to one another in psalms and hymns and spiritual songs, **singing and making melody in your heart to the Lord*** (Ephesians 5:19).

*Let the word of Christ dwell in you richly in all wisdom, teaching and admonishing one another in psalms and hymns and spiritual songs, **singing with grace in your hearts to the Lord*** (Colossians 3:16).

I would like to give you another testimony of how singing to the Lord brought victory in a desperate situation.

We were in Indonesia, preparing for a crusade, and the first problem that hit us was that my whole team became ill—everybody was sick. Then, one of the committee members came to me and said, "Sister Suzette, we must cancel the crusade, because the different denominations are boycotting us." I thought, *Dear Lord, we have just hired the stadium, and the sound system, paid for all the advertising, and a lot of other expenses, and now they come and tell me that we have to cancel. This is not right.*

Another committee came and said, "Sister Suzette, we have to cancel the morning seminars, because the Asian occult conference is taking place at the same time as our crusade, in the same building." (There was only one conference facility in this city.)

However, I found out that our conference was to be held on the top floor and the occult conference on the three lower floors! What an arrangement for spiritual warfare!

The next problem came from the police. They said that we should cancel the event, because a threat against our lives had been made, and they could not guarantee our security. It would be safer if we canceled the whole crusade.

I said to them, "Cancel? Cancel, because of an occult conference and a possible threat to our lives? Do we believe in 'He who was, who is, and is continuously present'? Do we believe that 'He is the same yesterday, today and forever'? If so, then we need to act accordingly." I told them, "It will be over my dead body that we cancel!"

I was so discouraged when I went to my room that I said, "God, I just can't do it. It is too much for me. I want to go home." The Holy Spirit then said to me, "Suzette, you know the answer." And then I asked Him to help me remember. At that moment, the precious Holy Spirit revealed it to me, and I understood—I needed to bring Him into the scene!

I closed my Bible, and began to worship Him. I started to sing a new song. I took the promises that God had given me for my life, and for my calling—the very Scriptures that I had been given. I took them all before the Lord in song and prayer. Out of the depth of my heart, alone in that bedroom with my team sick, with several denominations boycotting my crusade, with death threats against me, and an occult conference about to take place, I brought them all before the Lord, and I started singing the song of the Lord. I began to sing out of my spirit. I sang and sang, and faith rose up. So I sang some more. Inside of me, everything began to rise up, and suddenly, I came to a place of victory again.

I started praying, "The Spirit of the Lord is upon me to open prison doors, to set the captives free." And I started to *tehillah* before the Lord. I sang a word, or I prayed quietly. I read the Word of God out loud. As I *tehillah*-ed with Him, the power of God came. Faith comes by hearing and hearing the Word of the Lord.

Suddenly, there was a knock at my door, and there stood a man. God had sent this Catholic man to tell me that the Catholics had heard that I was in the city, and that they were going to broadcast my meetings live! Well, when the Pentecostals heard that the Catholics were going to broadcast the meetings, they decided that they too were going to broadcast them. And when the Evangelicals heard that the Catholics and Pentecostals were broadcasting the meetings, they too decided to get in on the act! By that night, I had a probable radio audience of 900,000. By the fourth night, 50,000 people had gathered in the stadium, and thousands were born again.

And then, my God began to heal people as they were listening to the radio! The power of the Word and *tehillah* changed defeat into victory. The next night, the testimonies came—tumors had disappeared, cripples walked, invalids recovered and got out of bed. One doctor came and said, "I am not a Christian.—I want to make that very clear. But this person is my patient and could not walk. Now, he walks."

The power of the Word combined with worship and prayer brings the One who was and is into the scene. Hallelujah!

Paul and Silas knew the power of prayer in song as well.

> *But at midnight Paul and Silas were praying and singing hymns to God, and the prisoners were listening to them. Suddenly there was a great earthquake, so that the foundations of the prison were shaken; and immediately all the doors were opened and everyone's chains were loosed (Acts 16:25-26).*

Paul and Silas lifted their voices in praise and worship, and He who was and is came at that moment and delivered them. There is not a prison door that can remain closed or a chain that can bind in the face of the power of worship. Let me give you some advice: *What prayer cannot get through, worship will.*

Allow me to share one further testimony with you of how I learned tephillah. I am not talking of singing the songs of some psalmists, but learning it for myself as a form of prayer before God.

I was ministering in a city in Germany, and we had one evening free on which I, and the team, accepted an invitation for a meal from a couple who had always attended our meetings. He was blind, and they lived in a center for handicapped people. These people were very precious to me, and we often had contact with them. Arriving at the home, a wonderful spread was put out for us with several of their friends of the same home attending. One of the ladies was so severely handicapped that she could hardly utter a full sentence in German. However, they all were born-again children of God.

At the end of the meal, my blind friend pushed back his chair and said, "Let's pray." The team and I bowed our heads, and softly started praying in tongues…but not these people. Our friend pushed back his chair and with a strong voice, he started singing his prayer and songs before God! The room filled with the presence of God. This was nothing new for them; it was clear that this was a lifestyle.

Meanwhile, the lady who could not even utter one sentence, suddenly opened her mouth and started singing a prayer in perfect German for about two minutes. I wept like a child. God had to take Suzette Hattingh, who had led thousands of people in prayer for years, to a group of handicapped people, in order to learn how to pray by song! The lady who sang that prayer prayed the most wonderful prayer that I have ever heard. She prayed prophetically, or rather, sang prophetically, her prayer for me. No one has ever prayed for me like that. I learned the power of *tephillah* as a lifestyle from them. Now, I practice this under all circumstances and for all circumstances.

Why Should You Sing?

Isaiah has a timely word for this world and its problems.

"Sing, O barren, you who have not borne! Break forth into singing, and cry aloud, you who have not labored with child! For more are the children of the desolate than the children of the married woman," says the Lord (Isaiah 54:1).

Some topics to sing about include:

- Sing to the barrenness of your church.
- Sing to the barrenness of your harvest.
- Sing to the barrenness of your marriage.
- Sing to the barrenness of your finances.
- Sing to the barrenness of your city.

Why should you sing?

You should sing, because "more are the children of the desolate than the children of those who are married." It is all spiritual.

Why should you sing?

So that you can enlarge to the north, south, east, and west; so that you can enlarge the place of your tent, and take the desolate cities for the Most High God.

What should you sing?

Sing the Word of the Lord back to Him; sing the prophetic words that you have already received, or simply sing your own words and prayer before the Lord.

> *Let us tehillah before God.*
> *Let us open our mouths and sing the song of the Lord.*
> *Let us sing unto the Lord in whatever form.*

CHAPTER 10

The Ministry of Support— Practical Application for Churches and Home Groups

HAVE YOU EVER WONDERED WHY some meetings seem to flow in the spirit and others do not? Why is it that, when the meeting flows in the spirit, the congregation goes home rejoicing and light in spirit; but when there seems to be resistance or a heaviness, then they are robbed of their joy? Oh, they talk and laugh after the meeting, but that lightness is not there.

Or have you ever wondered why sometimes you feel that you cannot "get on" with certain people? There appears to be no reason; they are very kind people, yet there is restraint there.

Or more specifically, have you ever wondered how you could be more effective for God, while sitting on the church pew, when you are not part of the fivefold ministry?

If you have ever wondered about these three points, then this chapter is just for you!

In this final chapter, we will consider "Kingdom mentality," which, as far as I am concerned, means "Body of Christ" mentality!

THE KINGDOM OF GOD IS SPIRITUAL AND IS DISCERNED SPIRITUALLY

*But **seek first the kingdom of God** and His righteousness, and all these things shall be added to you* (Matthew 6:33).

The Kingdom of God is such a vast concept and yet so explicit. The Greek word for "Kingdom" is *basileia*, which means a "state of being ruled with sovereignty, royal power, or dominion."

First, this Kingdom is not determined by observation. It does not occur in the natural realm, because it is a *spiritual* Kingdom. It is within us, and it is a mystery to non-Christians.

> *Now when He was asked by the Pharisees when the kingdom of God would come, He answered them and said, "The kingdom of God does not come with observation; nor will they say, 'See here!' or 'See there!' For indeed, **the kingdom of God is within you**"* (Luke 17:20-21).

> *And He said to them, "To you it has been given to know the mystery of the kingdom of God; but **to those who are outside, all things come in parables**"* (Mark 4:11).

The most wonderful thing about the Kingdom of God is that God said we could and would know it. We can know about it, we can understand it, and it can be very clear to us.

Second, knowledge concerning Kingdom matters is discerned spiritually; this is of great importance.

> *But the natural man does not receive the things of the Spirit of God, for they are foolishness to him; nor can he know them, because they are **spiritually discerned**** (1 Corinthians 2:14).

The man without the Holy Spirit does not accept the things that come from the Spirit of God, for they are foolishness to him, and he cannot understand them.

I truly believe that discernment is vital for intercession. I do not know how I could ever have flowed or continue to flow in ministry without this spiritual discernment. In this context, when I use either the word *discernment* or *discerning*, I am not referring to the gift of discerning spirits—that is something different. I mean that type of discernment whereby the Lord allows you to see with His eyes or to feel the way that He feels concerning a situation. Or more generally, to feel either a peace or joy about a certain situation, an inner withdrawal, or an unsettledness. It implies "determining the excellence or defects of a person or thing."

However, this discernment is not given to you so that you can judge that person or situation, but to appreciate what is necessary, as you stand in the gap for that person or event.

I can truly say that I generally operate in this type of discernment, but it has not always been the case. Rather, it has been a process of making mistakes and learning to hear the voice of God. To me, discernment is like the telephoto lens of a camera. At first, everything is in the picture, but as you zoom in, the picture becomes specific and focused. The Holy Spirit will soon warn us, or acquaint us with the fact that something is either right or wrong. And yet, there might not be anything wrong with the person or situation; it simply might not be what the Lord has for you at that particular time, or it might not be part of your destiny. It is here that absolute obedience to the Holy Spirit is paramount.

For example, a businessman suggests that the two of you go into a certain business venture together. He may be a born-again, blessed, dedicated man of prayer—everything that you have been looking for. Nevertheless, there is a little uneasiness in your spirit. Obey that warning! No matter how attractive the future might seem, how positive the plans appear, or how tempting the challenge, resist it with all your might! Otherwise, later, you will pay the consequences of overruling the Holy Spirit.

For the first few times that this happened to me, I kept saying, "Lord, what is wrong with me? How can I feel this way about this person, or even have these thoughts?" I soon learned that God was looking at the heart, and could see what I could not. There might not be anything wrong with another person, and yet your Father knows that your two personalities would not make for the best combination, and so He warns you. If that warning is obeyed, then the friendship will remain; if that warning is sidelined, then you might find that the company does not prosper, no matter how hard you work. Discernment warned you, but you overruled!

This kind of discernment is vital for prayer concerning the spiritual impact in a meeting. I can normally tell by the flow or discernment in my spirit, when I pray during my preparation time, how that meeting will turn out. It has proved to be one of the most powerful tools in my preparation time as to how to pray for that meeting. Do I sense a breakthrough and joy, or do I sense resistance? I then pray accordingly. Do I sense that the main flow of the meeting will be on the preaching of the Word? I then cut the preliminaries short and concentrate on the preaching. Do I sense that the main breakthrough will be during the ministry time afterwards? Then I preach, cut it short, and give extra time to the ministry time.

This is also very helpful when people come in to disturb a meeting. The Lord knows if there are people who have come into the meeting specifically to disrupt the preacher and whether witches are present to try to curse or release evil forces over the meeting. A child of God need have no fear of these actions.

A curse without cause shall not alight (Proverbs 26:2b).

The Spirit of God has warned me on many occasions about these matters. I had no physical proof of their presence, but discernment was in the spirit, and I was made aware of the situation.

I remember one meeting, when we were praying, the Spirit of God spoke to my heart and said, "Witches have just walked into the intercession hall." This hall had about 500 to 600 people praying, while the Word of God was preached during the crusade. As the Holy Spirit spoke to me, I looked up, and found that several of the prayer warriors who, minutes before were either kneeling down or laying flat on their faces praying, also looked up. They were aware that evil had walked in. We all had heard in our spirits the same word—"Witches have just walked in." We soon found those witches and dealt with the situation. That is discernment!

Consider the person who sat next to you last Sunday in church. At the time, you wondered why you felt so funny that you almost felt bound and anxious—that was your discernment. It was God telling you that the person next to you was not sent by Him to your place of worship. That is your discernment at work, and it is vitally important that you do not overrule or disregard it. It is also equally important not to become judgmental, or to look for faults with everybody, and, most importantly, not to fear, but to act productively. Start praying in tongues and begin to intercede for that person next to you. If your discernment is correct, this person will soon become uncomfortable and probably leave, or try to sit somewhere else. If your discernment is wrong, your prayers and intercession will only bless them. So no matter which way, it is a winning situation when you turn your discernment into prayer.

BODY MENTALITY

Having looked at discernment, we now want to connect it to the Kingdom mentality, and how it actually works there.

When we talk about Kingdom mentality, we are talking about an enlarged vision, about the place in which you are actually ruling over forces of darkness. It is about lining up our priorities with God's priorities, and considering the whole Body of Christ.

It is this aspect of the Body of Christ and the "Body mentality" that I want to focus upon. It is of the utmost importance that as members of the Body of Christ, we concern ourselves with the functioning of that Body.

I believe in revival, and I remember on one occasion, as I was ministering in a certain country, I was praying continuously for revival in that country. One morning, the Lord spoke to me. "Revival in this country will not come through one man. It will come only through the Body of Christ."

Why is that? It is because God is prepared to pour out His blessings in such a way that one man cannot handle it. I really believe that! He needs the whole Body to come together, in order to minister to all the "newborn babes." The whole Body must learn to minister to the sick and participate in what the Lord is doing. Just as when a natural flood strikes, two or three buckets are not sufficient to remove all the water, so it is when the flood of blessings arrives—the whole Body must participate.

In the Old Testament, the Holy Spirit moved upon the individual; whereas, in the New Testament, the Spirit of God has been poured out upon all flesh, which is the Church. For example, in the Book of Acts, the entire Church made intercession for Peter.

THE WHOLE BODY MUST LEARN TO MINISTER TO THE SICK AND PARTICIPATE IN WHAT THE LORD IS DOING.

*Peter was therefore kept in prison, but **constant prayer was offered to God for him by the church*** (Acts 12:5).

I firmly believe that the Body of Christ has been robbed of a wonderful move of prayer by allowing satan to box in intercession or persuade us that intercession is for only a few select people. At other times, we turn intercession into a mere "prayer meeting"! This is not right. Yes, a certain few are called to give themselves more to prayer than the rest, but God intended intercession to be practiced by the whole Church, for the whole Church!

INTERCESSION IS AS MUCH A PART OF THE LIFESTYLE IN CHRIST AS WORSHIP IS.

I cannot help but put the reason for this problem at the door of preachers and teachers. If we would teach young Christians from the day that they are saved that intercession is as much a part of the lifestyle in Christ as worship is, then our prayer meetings would look, and be, different. We point out the intercessors in the Old Testament, but exclude the principle of all-inclusiveness in the New Testament.

We have made intercession an end in itself, instead of a means to an end. If the Church would pray more, then the spiritual prisons would soon be empty. If the whole Church cried out in interceding prayer, then a mighty outpouring of the Spirit of God would be manifest throughout the nations, and an unimagined revival would occur. Kingdom mentality means coming out of yourself or your personal situation and interceding in partnership with the Body of Christ, irrespective of doctrinal positions, for the lost and needy of this world for whom Jesus has paid the price.

THE MINISTRY OF SUPPORT

Do you ever wonder what you can do for God? This chapter is for you. You can be extremely effective even though you are not a preacher or in the fivefold ministry. Once again, God taught me through a practical experience.

One day in a church meeting, at which I was a guest, I looked around and thought, *how heavy and restrained this meeting feels.* There was great oppression; the worship did not flow, and most everyone looked and felt tired. I watched the pastor praying as he waited for his turn to take the microphone. As he got up to bring the Word of God, I thought to myself, *Brother, I wonder how you are going to break through this meeting today.* At that instant, the Holy Spirit spoke to me, and said, "I hold you just as responsible as the preacher for ensuring the flow of the anointing in this meeting." I said, "Oh, no, Lord. I am just a visitor here." We really know how to argue with the Holy Spirit when it suits us! But, He knows how to win! He replied, "Is not this My house?" I said, "*Yes, Lord.*" He said, "Is that not My blood-washed son there?" I said, "Yes, Lord." He said, "Is this not the Body?" I said, "Yes, Lord." He said, "Are you not part of the Body?" I said, "Yes, Lord!" He then said, "Are you still a visitor?"

I grabbed my Bible and made a beeline for the prayer room!

At that moment, I learned that I am just as responsible for what happens in a meeting as the man who is preaching. "But, Suzette," you say, "you are an intercessor!" You are an intercessor as well if you are a child of God and part of the Body of Christ. Intercession is for the entire Body of Christ, for the whole Church.

You, man of God, are just as responsible; you, sister, are just as responsible for what happens in a meeting at which you are present as the speaker, worship leader, or pastor leading that meeting. You do not believe that? Well then, let us look at what the Word of God has to say about it.

> *Now Amalek came and fought with Israel in Rephidim. And Moses said to Joshua, "Choose us some men and go out, fight with Amalek. Tomorrow I will stand on the top of the hill with the rod of God in my hand." So Joshua did as Moses said to him, and fought with Amalek. And Moses, Aaron, and Hur went up to the top of the hill. And so it was, when Moses held up his hand, that Israel prevailed; and when he let down his hand, Amalek prevailed. But Moses' hands became heavy; so they took a stone and put it under him, and he sat on it. And Aaron and Hur supported his hands, one on one side, and the other on the other side; and his hands were steady until the going down of the sun. So Joshua defeated Amalek and his people with the edge of the sword* (Exodus 17:8-13).

I have often been to meetings at which the Word of God was preached in power, with signs and wonders following in accordance with the biblical principle, and what a wonderful experience it was. But at the very next meeting, there were difficulties. The same preacher, the same anointing, but the flow was like a trickle. How could this happen? The fact is, we are in a spiritual battle, whether we want to believe it or not. That does not mean that we have to be satan-conscious all the time, but neither does it mean that we must underestimate his tactics. I must think of what I can do to help and learn how to pray accordingly. This type of prayer brought me into one of the greatest releases in understanding the ministry of support, and I know that it will do the same for you. So, let me share with you a testimony how God led me further into it.

Once again, I was at a church meeting at which there was a fixed format of doing things. They worshipped, took up an offering, and listened to the Word of God, which was followed by an altar call. After the altar call was given, the service was formally closed. Everybody could go home, except those who stayed behind for ministry. As the altar call was given, I thought to myself, *Hmm, an early finish today*, and began to make my way out of the building, thinking about what I could have for lunch! When I reached the church door, the Holy Spirit said to me, "What are you doing?" What a strange question, I thought, and replied, "Nothing." "Exactly!" was His reply.

At that precise moment, when the greatest battle was being fought, when satan was trying his best to convince people not to give their lives to Jesus, because their friends would laugh at them, their spouse would not agree, or a million and one other reasons for not doing anything rash—at that very moment, I was heading out of the church thinking only about some lunch! What was the local Body of Christ doing? What was the army of God doing? They were doing just what I had replied to the Holy Spirit—nothing!

Instead of Kingdom mentality, we had selfish mentality; instead of considering the warfare in the heavenlies, we were considering our stomachs. Passive Christianity, not active Christianity, is the scourge of the modern Church. This, however, was not the attitude of either Amalek or Israel.

> PASSIVE CHRISTIANITY, NOT ACTIVE CHRISTIANITY, IS THE SCOURGE OF THE MODERN CHURCH.

Amalek, in Exodus chapter 17, is a type of the church's enemy, namely the forces of darkness, whereas Israel is a type for the active Church of Jesus Christ, comprising you, me, and every other born-again child of God. Aaron and Hur typify prayer warriors. I want to draw your attention to the fact that the victory was not dependent upon Joshua, although he was the one leading the army. Joshua did the physical battle, but the victory depended upon Moses!

WHEN MOSES'
HANDS WERE HELD UP
HIGH, THE WHOLE OF
ISRAEL PREVAILED.

While his hands were up in the air, what happened? Was it just a victory for Moses, Aaron, and Hur? Was it just a victory for one or two people? No. The Word of God says that the whole of Israel prevailed. This is a significant point, and one that must be understood. When Moses' hands were held up high, *the whole of Israel prevailed.* However, when his arms grew weary and sank to his side, the Amalekites were victorious. It was defeat not just for Moses, Aaron, and Hur, but also for the whole of the Israelite nation. Everyone was involved.

Now, consider your own meetings. Think of the time that the man of God preached under a powerful anointing, and the Spirit of God moved on the people. You all went home uplifted and rejoicing at such a wonderful meeting. But what about the days when things did not go as well? The days, for want of better words, which were not so blessed, which were not so free and exciting. What happened? The same pastor preached; the same crowd of people were present. Did these thoughts pass through your mind—*I wonder what was wrong with the pastor? Was he sick? He just could not get it together!* We all have had these types of thoughts when a meeting does not appear to flow smoothly.

If only you had Kingdom mentality that day, you would have grasped the fact that satan had come in with more forces, in order to disrupt the service, to withhold the Word of God from you, and to dampen your enthusiasm for the Lord. Kingdom mentality is rising from your own position, looking into the spirit realm, and understanding what is happening there. That day, when things did not go so easily, was the very day that God needed you on your spiritual feet. That was the day God needed you to rise against the forces of darkness, and to support the preacher through intercession. Wherever you were sitting, either in the congregation or on the platform, by praying in tongues quietly to yourself while he was preaching, you would have been blessed by the message, and your spirit would have been actively engaged in Kingdom mentality.

When are our modern-day equivalents to Moses on their feet? It is certainly not at the breakfast table; neither is it later in the evening, when they are having supper at home! No! It is when they are preaching the Word of God. It is when they are in the pulpit exhorting the flock. That is the time at which satan launches his attack against the shepherds of the Church. He already has his spiritual artillery sighted on the pulpits and rostrums in every active church, so that as soon as a preacher approaches that area, there is a mighty spiritual barrage against the Word of God. At that very moment, in the heavenlies, there is the greatest battle taking place to withhold the revelation and understanding of the Word of God from your spirit, your mind, and the Church as a whole, through distraction, disturbance, or simply resistance.

SATAN ATTACKS THE PREACHING OF THE WORD OF GOD.

SUPPORTING THE ROD OF GOD

I now want to focus upon the rod, which Moses carried. Exodus 17:9b states:

*Tomorrow I will stand on the top of the hill with the **rod of God in my hand**.*

Neither Aaron the high priest, nor Hur attempted to take that rod out of the hands of Moses. What they did *was to support the hand that held the rod!* Children of God, when our elders and leaders (our modern types of Moses) are holding up their authoritative rod of God, which for us is the Word of God, that is the time they need you to uphold their hands. Moses became weary, and often, it is exactly the same situation in the Church. I know what I am talking about. I am a preacher of the Word of God myself, yet how many times, while preaching, have I thought to myself, *Oh my God, if only someone were praying for me now?* It is for this very reason that I thank God for each and every one of my coworkers, because every moment that I minister the Word of God, they are praying for me, they are supporting me, they are upholding my hands in the spirit realm. Even though they are sitting in the front row, enjoying the Word of God, they are still active in prayer in their spirits.

The rod of God remained in the hands of Moses; they did not try to take it out of his hands. And the same applies to us. We are not trying to rule, control, or demand; we are not trying to change the message; we are not trying to change our leaders. Rather, we are there to support them. Whether you agree with what they do or not, God has put

GOD HAS PUT YOUR LEADERS IN A POSITION OF AUTHORITY FOR A PURPOSE.

them there, and put them there for a purpose. Intercession is a supportive ministry! It is neither your task nor mine to deal with the leaders in correction; that is God's work. We cannot control them with our prayers, because that is spiritual witchcraft. We are there to pray for them and to leave it to the Holy Spirit to deal with it in His way.

"Oh, sister, you don't know my pastor; you don't know this man." That is true—I do not know him, but Jesus knows him very well. And He has put him in that position. *We have no right to try to take the rod out of his hand.*

A further point, to which I want to draw your attention, is the fact that Aaron and Hur brought the stone to Moses. They did not try to move Moses to the stone; *they brought the stone to him!* They did not try to change his position, his vision, or his view of the conflict. They supported him where he had positioned himself. This aspect is very important. We must support the church leadership at the place where they are already situated.

WE MUST SUPPORT THE CHURCH LEADERSHIP AT THE PLACE WHERE THEY ARE ALREADY SITUATED.

That day, when the ministry was not flowing the way you thought it should, was also the day of your failure. It was not only the failure of the shepherd; *it was your failure as well*, because we are a body. When my head has a blackout, or something happens to my brain, it affects my entire body. It is the same in the Body of Christ. If the leaders are affected, then we too become affected.

DO NOT LIMIT YOUR VISION TO YOUR OWN SPECIFIC AREA OF MINISTRY

Let us now consider Aaron. Aaron was a priest. In fact, he was the high priest but what was the responsibility of a priest? The priest's responsibility was to minister unto the Lord, to carry the ark, and to burn incense before the Lord in the tabernacle. Now, do you know what Aaron could have done? Do you know what Moses could have done? They both could have legitimately said to Joshua, "Joshua, you go out and fight the battle tomorrow. We will wait here in the tent." Aaron could have said, "I will burn all the sacrifices, and I will burn offerings unto God, and burn sweet incense unto God, and make peace offerings. You fight the battle, and when you're done, send somebody to let us know what has happened." Moses could have said, "Joshua, you go and fight. I will stand here at the tent of God, and I will wait and listen if God has anything to say."

But the Bible tells it differently! They all targeted the same battle. They all took part according to their role. All four of them had an appointed task. If any one of them had failed in their allotted role, the whole mission would have failed! They all fought the same enemy at the same time. We need to fight at the same time—not each other, but the enemy.

When our "Moses" is on his feet, that is the time at which we must concentrate our maximum effort in order to foil the enemy plan of withholding the Word of God from the flock of Christ. I believe that every prayer meeting, every church meeting, every time the children of God come together—be it for the ministering of the Word, or be it for a prayer meeting—then we have an Exodus chapter 17 situation.

Neither Moses nor Aaron held on to their allotted role as leader of the nation and high priest, but joined in *together with* the army in the national conflict.

We see a similar situation with David and Goliath. Just as David fought Goliath, which is such a perfect example of natural as well as spiritual warfare, you bind the strongman and then spoil his house. David's victory became the victory of the entire Israeli army.

Let's consider the time that the preacher ministers the Word of God and is very much engaged in the spirit world as he ministers. Then consider the amount of passive time that the "listeners" spend, during that ministration of the Word. So many look solely at their own little position, their own little office, their own particular place in the order of service, and woe betide anyone who steps over that demarcation line! Lord, help us to look away from ourselves and unto Jesus, the author and finisher of our faith!

Let me give you an example of how I see many churches today. I will use the role of worship leader in this example, but I want to stress that this could apply to any other position. (I have nothing against worship leaders; this is simply a role I have chosen for this example.)

As the worship leaders lead the worship, they lead us into the holiest place, right into the presence of Almighty God. Then, when the worship time has finished, they put down their instruments and do not pick them up again until the final chorus. The next person comes, perhaps the treasurer with his report, followed by the taking of the offering; and after this, perhaps the notices for the week, eloquently read out by the secretary. There is absolutely nothing wrong with what is going on in the service, but what about the musicians? What about those who have just led us into the very presence of God? What are they doing in the meanwhile, or more significantly, what should they be doing, having laid down their instruments?

Once you have put down your instruments, you should continue flowing in the anointing. Do not limit your vision to your own specific area of ministry; continue to minister, but in a different way. As the meeting gets underway, pray in tongues or in your spirit. Do not simply hold onto the gift that God has given you, but move out into prayer, because we are still busy with warfare, with building the Kingdom, with what is happening in the spirit world; we still need to be part of all that. It is so easy to become a passive spectator, and yet we all have to be actively engaged in advancing Kingdom principles. Having done your allotted task, hand the responsibility over to the next minister, but *actively support him or her in prayer*.

The same applies to the treasurer and secretary, and all the members of the congregation. We all are part of a living body, and must act accordingly by inputting into that body. Now, when the pastor stands up to preach, the meeting is blessed and flows freely.

After the Word, maybe there is an altar call or ministry for the sick, but where is the rest of the body, apart from the few who are directly involved? They are outside chatting about this and that, all of which is inconsequential considering the spiritual battle that is taking place inside the building. This is the time for supporting the ministry team; this is the time for prayer both in the spirit and in the understanding. This is the time to become a shareholder and to be part of what is happening in the spiritual realm. This is definitely the time to be active and not passive, so that demons are cast out, the sick are healed, the lame walk, the blind see, the deaf have their ears opened, and all to the glory of God!

Once I understood this principle, I never again allowed myself to be passive. I pray for the man of God in the meeting, and because I am physically present, I am blessed with the rest of the congregation. I am excited; I am part of the message; I agree with the Word of God and am blessed by it. I sit and take my notes, just like everyone else, and yet all the time, I am praying in my spirit, *Yes Lord, I agree with that word. Let it touch the lives of people.* As I sit there listening and praying, I become a shareholder. In the spirit world, I become a part of what God is doing. I am upholding the hands of "Moses"; I am upholding the rod that is stretched out over the people; I am upholding the man of God ministering.

And do you know what? In the beginning, it was difficult, very difficult! I could not even pray for five minutes through the meeting. But the more I practiced, the easier it became; and the easier it became, the more it became part of my life.

THOSE WHO SUPPORTED OTHERS

Let us now look at a few more examples of the ministry of support, which are found in the Word of God.

> But Peter, **standing up with the eleven**, *raised his voice and said to them, "Men of Judea and all who dwell in Jerusalem, let this be known to you, and heed my words"* (Acts 2:14).

In Acts 2:14, Peter stood up with the eleven others. What was he doing? He was preaching. However, if ten of the eleven were not necessary, why did they stand up? They stood up in spiritual support of Peter! Their faith was as important for the breakthrough of that meeting as Peter's faith. To me, that is a New Testament example of the Old Testament principle found in Exodus chapter 17.

In Acts 3:4, Peter and John were on their way to the temple for afternoon prayers. At the Beautiful Gate sat a beggar. What did Peter say to him? He said. "Look at *us*." Who then continued the actions? It was Peter. Peter spoke to him, and lifted him up, and yet he had said, "Look at us." John was there as an active supporter.

In Judges 4:8, we meet with Deborah and Barak. Deborah was not the one holding a spear and a shield. It was not because of her weapon skills that Barak said to her, "If you will go with me, then I will go; but if you will not go with me, I will not go!" Rather, he was fully aware of the spiritual support that this woman could give to his army. Look at Deborah's attitude. In Judges 5:9 she said, "My heart is with the rulers of Israel who offered themselves willingly with the people. Bless the Lord!" She claimed no personal recognition. To me this is true spiritual support.

In Second Samuel 11:11, Uriah the Hittite identified himself with the battle that was taking place in the field. He told David,

> *The ark and Israel and Judah are dwelling in tents, and my lord Joab and the servants of my lord are encamped in the open fields. Shall I then go to my house to eat and drink, and to lie with my wife? As you live, and as your soul lives, I will not do this thing* (2 Samuel 11:11).

We Are Shareholders, Builders, and Soldiers

Let me ask you a question. If your pastor travels to a foreign country on mission work or goes across town to another place to preach, what do you do? If he travels abroad, the leaders usually gather round, pray for him, lay hands on him, and wish him, "Bon voyage." They then retire from the scene until he returns! At the time when he really needs prayer, most of the leaders will be either in front of the television or asleep in bed! What use is that? When he is away is the time that he needs you to support him by fasting and praying for him, because that is the time in which he will be dealing with even more forces of darkness than ever before. That is the time to become a Uriah and identify with your leader.

The ministry of support makes us shareholders in that which we are supporting. How do we know that? First Samuel 30:24 gives us the answer.

> *For who will heed you in this matter? But as his part is who goes down to the battle, so shall his part be who stays by the supplies;* **they shall share alike** (1 Samuel 30:24).

Please refer to Chapter 2, "The Harvest of Intercession," where this principle is discussed in detail.

The same thing happens in Joshua 22:8. For brevity, I will quote just the last section, "Divide the spoil of your enemies with your brethren." These quotations should encourage you to take up the ministry of support, and share in the spoils of the strongman.

Another facet of the ministry of support is the building of a wall of protection around the vulnerable. In Ezekiel 22:30, the Lord was looking for someone to build a wall.

> So I sought for a man among them who would make a wall, and stand in the gap before Me on behalf of the land, that I should not destroy it; but I found no one (Ezekiel 22:30).

In the rebuilding of Jerusalem, Nehemiah gathered his troops and builders together.

> So it was, from that time on, that half of my servants worked at construction, while the other half held the spears, the shields, the bows, and wore armor; and the leaders were behind all the house of Judah. Those who built on the wall, and those who carried burdens, loaded themselves so that with one hand they worked at construction, and with the other held a weapon (Nehemiah 4:16-17).

(As an aside, it is from this quotation that Charles Spurgeon took the name for his magazine—*The Sword and Trowel*.)

It is this type of situation that we must have today in the Church. While the work is taking place, while we are building the temple of God, we should also have our weapon in our hand. Soldiers are taught never to go anywhere without their weapon, and that includes going to bed!

Our wall of protection must be built in prayer. This is another of those very important points. Why is it important to build a wall of protective prayer? When witches and wizards come into meetings, they particularly want to disrupt the meeting, and they make every effort to get into the front rows, right in front of the preacher. From there, they have an open view of the man of God and can launch their wicked works. It is hard to believe that there are people in this world who would do such a thing, but sadly, it is a fact.

It is time to stop sitting on the back rows, so that we can get out quickly after the meeting. We must be at the front, in order to take the best places and to build a wall of protection around the stage, the podium, and the place of ministry.

In my case, the supportive ministry began many years ago during an African crusade. Pastor Reinhard Bonnke was preaching the Word of God. His entire team was on the stage; some were attentively listening, others were leafing through their Bibles, and so on. By now I had

IT IS TIME TO STOP SITTING AT THE BACK. WE MUST BE AT THE FRONT, TO BUILD A WALL OF PROTECTION AROUND THE PLACE OF MINISTRY.

learned to pray during the meetings, while the preacher was preaching, which is what I was doing. Suddenly, I had an open vision, and I saw a wall being built from me. I was virtually the corner stone from which that wall was built. In this vision, I could clearly see how the forces of darkness attacked, yet were blocked by the wall. And then the vision was gone.

I said nothing to anyone about it at the time, but was rather perplexed about what it could mean. After the meeting, we had tea together, and the man of God said, "Something strange happened to me tonight while I preached. I had such an awful headache that I could hardly think straight. I had difficulty concentrating on my preaching, when suddenly, the headache lifted as if cut with a knife." My ears picked up like antennas. *Could this be the vision?* I said to him, "Was it at this specific point of the sermon?" "Yes," he said. "How did you know?" As I related the vision, I realized that God was teaching me a spiritual principle that would radically change my life forever. I was learning the power of the supportive ministry!

PRACTICAL ADVICE

Consider dividing the prayers or intercessors of your church into different groups. Some can take the front rows on different Sundays, and others can pray parallel (contemporaneously), perhaps in another room.

If people are allowed to sit on the stage during a meeting, it is wise to position one or two prayers on the stage as well.

If people are praying parallel outside in a room, communication is vital. It is good for the intercession leader to go occasionally into the main meeting, in order to see how things are progressing, so that the intercessory prayers can be more effectively directed.

Position your prayers at crusades. You can pray just as effectively inside the meeting as outside. (Note that when you pray outside, you can express yourself more freely.) During an evangelistic outreach, or any other meeting for that matter, if at all possible, position one or two prayers on the stage, front row, and grandstands, if at all available. Teach your prayers not to draw attention to themselves, but to realize that it is not by might, nor by power, but by the Spirit of the Lord.

I very seldom travel alone. Usually, I travel with at least one of my team, no matter how young or old a Christian that person might be. Praying during the meeting for however long or short that person might be able to pray is a must. Not everybody has the passion for intercession, but everybody can be part of the supportive ministry, and become a shareholder in the rewards of that meeting.

Make the ministry of support a lifestyle and see yourself develop from strength to strength.

Epilogue

APPROACHING THE END OF THIS study, hopefully, you are now inspired to sharpen or deepen your personal lifestyle of prayer. Learning to pray what is on the Father's heart is not only a rich blessing for everyone who embarks on this adventure with the Lord, but it is also the greatest priority for the Church today.

May I briefly recall the most important principles that we have covered, in order to further motivate and encourage you to use this book as a handbook for everyday use, and to make prayer a practical, everyday practice.

First, prayer and intercession were never meant to be a sort of "specialization" for a selected group of people; rather, they are a great privilege and wonderful experience for every child of God, including you.

Looking at the biblical foundation of prayer and intercession, we discovered that our Bible is full of wonderful examples of intercessors who saw their environment change because of their prayer.

We also learned that worship, that place of intimacy with God, is the one and only basis of our prayer. It is there that we hear what is on God's heart and from there we start our intercessory prayer. I want to challenge you to be aware of the spiritual armor that you are wearing and to use it. Sometimes this might seem heavy, but God has given you His Holy Spirit, the best possible help, to come to your aid. And in Christ, nothing and nobody can touch you. Don't be afraid to start receiving a burden of God for your life and to learn to wage spiritual battle for the salvation of unbelievers, to pierce through like the point of a spear in a specific situation, and to intercede for your work, your city, or even your nation. Obey when the Spirit gives you an impulse burden for immediate intercession, or when He gives you a long-term burden for your family, your neighborhood, or church.

When we pray, we partner *together with* Jesus and the Holy Spirit. One of the most important principles is that you pray *hagah* the Word of God, because that will never return void or *without fruit*. When we pray like that, God will give breakthroughs in human lives and even in countries. However, this may well require *travail*—perseverance and strong determination in prayer, to call the vision we have received into existence. Always keep *praying your vision*, for it is an immeasurable privilege that Almighty God has chosen to use you and me to execute His will here on earth. Be open for this wonderful gift of prayer the Lord has for you.

Let's close our study and start our adventure by praying the following prayer of dedication:

> *Dear Father, thank You for teaching me so much about the power of prayer. Lord, I long to be used by You to make a difference in the lives of others, and subsequently I expect to reap a personal harvest of blessing as well. I yield my life to You. When You give me a prayer burden, I dedicate myself to be faithful and pray as You expect me to be available. I am aware that my prayer is a sustaining ministry to others who work in Your Kingdom, and I want to take my place. In this manner, Your Kingdom will expand, the Body of Christ will grow, and many will realize their need of salvation through Jesus Christ, Your Son. Thank You that I am a shareholder of these fruits! Dear Father, Your Kingdom come. Your will be done. As it is in Heaven, so be it on earth. Thank You for the privilege of using me. Amen!*

Contact the Author

Voice in the City
Suzette Hattingh Ministries

Address of our UK-office:

Voice in the City
PO Box 5836
Halesowen West Midlands
B63 3HF
United Kingdom
Tel: + 44 (0)121 602 4545

Address of our German office:

Voice in the City
Postfach 620140
60350 Frankfurt am Main
Germany
Tel: + 49 (0)69 426 909 0

info@voiceinthecity.org
www.voiceinthecity.org

Additional copies of this book and other book titles from DESTINY IMAGE™ EUROPE are available at your local bookstore.

We are adding new titles every month!

To view our complete catalog online, visit us at:
www.eurodestinyimage.com

Send a request for a catalog to:

Via Acquacorrente, 6
65123 - Pescara - ITALY
Tel. +39 085 4716623 - Fax +39 085 9431270

"Changing the world, one book at a time."

Are you an author?

Do you have a "today" God-given message?

CONTACT US

We will be happy to review your manuscript for a possible publishing:

publisher@eurodestinyimage.com